PSYCHOPATH FREE

Recovering from Emotionally Abusive
Relationships With Narcissists, Sociopaths,
& Other Toxic People

by PEACE

Dedicated to the Constants in my life – Thank you for restoring my faith in the goodness of people.

"No hurt survives for long without our help,
she said & then she kissed me & sent me out to play
again for the rest of my life."

Brian Andreas

INTRODUCTION
An Adventure

Psychopathy is an adventure, that's for sure. It will open your eyes to human nature, our broken society, and perhaps most important of all: your own spirit. It's a dark journey that will throw you into spells of depression, rage, and loneliness. It will unravel your deepest insecurities, leaving you with a lingering emptiness that haunts your every breath.

But ultimately, it will heal you.

You will become stronger than you could ever imagine. You will understand who you are truly meant to be. And in the end, you will be glad it happened.

No one ever believes me about that last part. At least, not at first. But I promise you, it's an adventure worth taking. One that will change your life forever.

At PsychopathFree.com, we see new members join every single day, always with a seemingly hopeless & all-too-familiar tale. Often on the brink of suicide, they wonder if they will ever find happiness again.

One year later, that person is nowhere to be found.

In their place, a beautiful stranger who stands tall and helps others out from the shadows. A stranger who takes pride in their own greatest qualities: empathy, compassion, and kindness. A stranger who speaks of self-respect and boundaries. A stranger who practices introspection in order to better conquer their own demons.

So what happened in that year?

Well, a lot of good stuff. So much that I had to write a book. I might be biased—actually, I definitely am—but I think PsychopathFree has one of the coolest healing processes out there. We believe in education, open dialog, validation, and self-discovery. We have a uniquely inspiring user base, full of resilient values and honest friendships.

Yes, friendships. Because this journey is personal, but it's also remarkably universal. Whether it be a whirlwind romance, an abusive marriage, or a life-consuming affair, the end result is always the same. Your mind is left spinning. You feel worthless and lost. You become numb to the things that once made you happy.

I cannot fix any of that, but I can give you a new place to start. And I can promise that you will feel joy again. You will learn to trust your intuition. You will walk this world with the wisdom of a survivor & the gentle wonder of a dreamer.

But first, you'll need to forget everything you thought you knew about people. Understanding psychopathy requires letting go of your basic emotional instincts. Remember, these are people who prey on forgiveness. They thrive on your need for closure. They manipulate compassion and exploit sympathy.

Since the dawn of time, psychopaths have waged psychological warfare on others—humiliating and shaming kind, unsuspecting victims. People who never asked for it. People who aren't even aware of the war until it's over.

But this is all about to change.

So say farewell to love triangles, cryptic letters, self-doubt, and manufactured anxiety. You will never again find yourself desperately awaiting a text from the person you love. You will never again censor your spirit for fear of losing the perfect relationship. You will never again be told to stop over-analyzing that which urgently needs analysis. You are no longer a pawn in the mind games of a psychopath. You are free.

And now, it's time for your adventure.

Love,

Peace

SPOTTING TOXIC PEOPLE

Your strengthened intuition is a psychopath's worst night-mare. It is a skill that can never be manipulated—and once learned, it will serve you a lifetime.

30 Red Flags

There are a lot of phenomenal studies on the traits and characteristics of psychopaths. For professional research, check out Cleckley's criteria or Hare's psychopathy checklist. A quick Google search ought to do the trick. The red flags in this book are intended to supplement those resources.

So what's different about this list? Well, for one, it's specifically about relationships. But it's also about **you**. Each point requires introspection and self-awareness. Because if you want to spot toxic people, you cannot focus entirely on their behavior—that's only half the battle. You must also come to recognize the looming red flags in your own heart. Then, you will be ready for anything.

1. **You feel on-edge around this person, but you still want them to like you.** You find yourself writing off most of their questionable behavior as accidental or in-sensitive, because you're in constant competition with

others for their attention and praise. They don't seem to care when you leave their side—they can just as easily move on to the next source of energy.

2. **Uses sex as a tool for control**. After first hooking you with sexual praise and flattery, they suddenly become reclusive and uninterested. They make you feel desperate, ensuring that you are always the one to initiate physical intimacy. They use insulting names like "whore" and "slut" to drive this point home. They might also openly comment on their diminishing sex drive.

3. **Plasters your Facebook page with compliments, flattery, songs, and poems**. They text you dozens, if not hundreds of times per day. You come to rely on this over-communication as a source of confidence.

4. **Quickly declares you their soul mate**. And for some reason, you don't find it creepy. They tell you how much they have in common with you. On the first few dates, you do most of the talking and they just can't believe how perfect you are for them.

5. **Compares you to everyone else in their life**. Ex-lovers, friends, family members, and your eventual replacement. When idealizing, they make you feel special by telling you how much better you are than these people. When devaluing, they use these comparisons to hurt you.

6. **Lies & excuses**. There is always an excuse for everything, even things that don't require excusing. They make up lies faster than you can question them. They will al-

ways blame others—it is never their fault. They spend more time rationalizing their behavior than improving it.

7. **Eternal boredom**. No startle response. Total absence of anxiety, fear, and worry where there otherwise should be. Very easily uninterested by the familiar. You write this off as calm and cool, often feeling inferior and over-sensitive because you have normal human emotions.

8. **Insults you with a condescending, joking sort of attitude**. Smirks when you try to express yourself. Teasing becomes the primary mode of communication in your relationship. They subtly belittle your intelligence and achievements. If you point this out, they call you hyper-sensitive and crazy.

9. **Uses social networking to provoke jealousy and rivalries while maintaining their cover of innocence**. They once focused all of their attention on you, but now they post ambiguous videos and statuses to make you doubt your place in their heart. They bait previously denounced exes with old songs and inside jokes. They attend to the "competition's" activity and ignore yours.

10. **You find yourself playing detective**. It's never happened in any other relationship, but suddenly you're scrolling back years on their Facebook page and albums. Same with their ex. You're seeking answers to a feeling you can't quite explain.

11. **Surrounds themselves with former lovers and potential mates**. Brags that they all want to sleep with him/her, but assures you there is nothing to worry about.

These people make you feel jealous and give off the perception that the psychopath is in high-demand.

12. **Hyperbolizes emotions while displaying none of them**. They make passionate statements like "I've never felt so happy in my life" in a completely robotic voice. It sounds like an alien trying to explain how they imagine human emotions might feel.

13. **You are the only one who sees their true colors.** Others will think they're the nicest person in the world, even though they are used for money, resources, and attention. They won't care because he/she strategically distracts them with shallow praise (often done over social networking). Psychopaths are able to maintain superficial friendships far longer than their relationships.

14. **Accuses you of emotions that they are intentionally provoking**. They will call you jealous after blatantly flirting with their ex over social networking for the world to see. They will call you needy after intentionally ignoring you for three days straight.

15. **Cannot put themselves in your shoes, or anyone else's for that matter**. You find yourself desperately trying to explain how they might feel if you were treating them this way, and they just stare at you blankly.

16. **You are engaged in constant conversations about their ex**. You know them by name, and you know everything about their relationship—at least, your partner's version of events. The ex becomes one of the most frequent topics of discussion in your relationship.

17. **You find yourself explaining the basic elements of human respect to a full-grown man/woman**. Normal people understand the fundamental concepts of honesty and kindness. No adult should need to be told how they are making other people feel.

18. **Focuses on your mistakes and ignores their own**. If they're two hours late, don't forget that you were once five minutes late to your first date. If you point out their inappropriate behavior, they will always be quick to turn the conversation back on you.

19. **Suddenly and completely bored by you**. Gives you the silent treatment and becomes very annoyed that you seem to be interested in continuing the passionate relationship that they created. You are now a chore to them.

20. **The ultimate hypocrite**. They have extremely high expectations for fidelity, respect, and adoration. After the idealization phase, they will give none of this back to you. They will cheat, lie, insult, and manipulate. But you are expected to remain perfect.

21. **Sometimes it seems as though they've forgotten who they're supposed to be around you**. They adopt different personas for different people—transforming their entire personality to match various audiences. It's always very eerie when they slip and accidentally use the wrong mask for you. You will start to feel that their personality just doesn't seem to add up.

22. **An unusual amount of "crazy" people in their past**. Any ex-partner or friend who did not come crawling

back to them will likely be labeled jealous, bipolar, an alcoholic, or some other nasty smear. They will speak about you the same way to their next target.

23. **Flatters your deepest insecurities**. If you're self-conscious about your looks, they'll call you the sexiest person in the world. If you've got a need to entertain, they'll say you're the funniest person they've ever known. They will also mirror your greatest fantasies, playing whatever role is necessary to win your heart.

24. **Frequently comments about what you're wearing and how you look**. They try to arrange you. You become obsessed with your appearance, noticing flaws that likely don't even exist. During and after the relationship, you will spend significantly more time in front of the mirror. (Thank you to our member, ckwanderlust, for these valuable insights).

25. **You fear that any fight could be your last**. Normal couples argue to resolve issues, but psychopaths make it clear that negative conversations will jeopardize the relationship, especially ones regarding their behavior. You apologize and forgive quickly, otherwise you know they'll lose interest in you.

26. **Obsessed with humiliating successful, kind & cheerful people**. Delighted by the idea of breaking up friendships and marriages. If you work hard to maintain interpersonal peace in your life, they will make it their mission to uproot all of it.

27. **Gaslighting**. Blatantly denies their own manipulative behavior and ignores evidence when confronted with it. They will become angry if you attempt to disprove their delusions with facts.

28. **They expect you to read their mind**. If they stop communicating with you for several days, it's your fault for not knowing about the plans they never told you about. There will always be a self-victimizing excuse to go along with this.

29. **Selfishness and a crippling thirst for attention**. They drain the energy from you and consume your entire life. Their demand for adoration is insatiable. You thought you were the only one who could make them happy, but now you feel that anyone with a beating pulse could fit the role. However, the truth is: no one can fill the void of a psychopath's soul.

30. **Your feelings**. After a run-in with a psychopath, you will feel insane, exhausted, drained, shocked, suicidal, and empty. You will tear apart your entire life—spending money, ending friendships, and searching for some sort of reason behind it all.

You will find that normal, loving people do not raise any of these flags. After an encounter with a psychopath, most survivors face the struggle of hypervigilance: who can really be trusted? Your gauge will swing back and forth for a while, like a volatile pendulum. You will wonder if you've gone absolutely mad—wanting to believe the best in an old friend or a new date, but feeling sick to the stomach when you actually spend time with them.

Developing your intuition is a personal process, but I would leave you with this: the world is mostly full of good people, and you don't want to miss out on that because you've been hurt. Spend some time getting in touch with your feelings. Keep tweaking until you find a comfortable balance of awareness and trust. Look within and understand why you felt the way you did. You will discover that many old relationships may need revisiting. And as you begin to abandon toxic patterns, healthier ones will inevitably appear in their place.

To quote a longtime member & friend, Phoenix, you will stop asking "Do they like me?" and start asking "Do I like them?"

Beware the Vultures

I'd like to extend a special warning to those of you who are new to recovery. After psychopathic abuse, you're going to be extremely raw and vulnerable. As you start to put the pieces together, you'll feel devastated, miserable, and angry. It's overwhelming.

You're probably used to repressing your emotions and dealing with things on your own. But this time, everything is out in the open. You're dependent like a newborn child, seeking out someone—anyone—to understand what you're going through.

In general, it's important to be open with your emotions. But at your most insecure moments, you often unknowingly open the floodgates for more abuse.

It's no mystery that survivors seem to attract more pathological people like magnets. As you frantically share your story, you latch onto the quickest & most sympathetic ear—anyone who claims to understand you. The problem is, these people do not always have your best interests at heart.

Those willing to listen to your psychopathic story for hours on end are, unfortunately, not likely to be people who are truly invested in your recovery.

Vultures often seem exceptionally kind and warm at first. They want to fix you and absorb your problems. They are fascinated by your struggles. But sooner or later, you will find yourself lost in another nightmare. They begin drowning you in unsolicited advice. They need constant praise and attention. You are never allowed to disagree with them. They feed off of drama and an insatiable need to be appreciated by others.

You will find that they lash out as you become happier. They perceive your progress as a threat to their control. They want to keep you in a perpetual state of co-dependency. They do not want you to seek help from anyone except them.

Pathological or not, you don't need this toxic garbage after what you've been through.

I would strongly urge all survivors to avoid seeking out new friendships and relationships for at least a few months. You must get to the point where you no longer need—or want—to talk about the psychopath anymore.

When you do need help, stick to professional therapy or recovery forums & services. These people know what you've been through, and you're going to find that all of them are willing to help—with no strings attached.

I understand the temptation to go out and meet new people. You're looking to start rebuilding your life. You want to surround yourself with kinder and more genuine friends.

And you will.

But real friends won't be acting as your therapist, and they definitely won't be rambling on about their ability to empathize & care. Their actions should speak louder than their words.

It takes a long time to start building healthier relationships. It takes breaking old habits, forming new ones, developing your intuition, and finally coming to understand what it is that you want from this world.

The Constant

You know about psychopaths. You've got the red flags. So now, the big question: how do you protect yourself?

Well, barring any major scientific advancements, you really can't know for certain whether or not someone has a conscience. In fact, I don't think there's any approach that will allow you to spot a psychopath with 100% confidence.

Fortunately, there's a different way to keep yourself safe. And this one involves looking within. It will work with anyone, anywhere, anytime. It's a question with answers—lots of them.

"How are you feeling today?"

Seriously, I'm asking you. Because most people might respond with a casual comment about their weekend, a promotion at work, or their favorite television show.

But what about you? Perhaps you're feeling empty? Broken? Hopeless? Maybe you woke up with that constant aching in your heart, eating away at your soul like a cancer. You spend the day trying to keep your thoughts free from painful topics—only to find that your mind keeps racing right back to them. Memories that once brought you so much joy now make you feel sick. You oscillate between anger and depression because you are unable to decide which one hurts less.

Those are answers.

So when you feel those things after a relationship, does it really matter if your ex was a psychopath, a sociopath, a narcissist, or a garden-variety jerk? The label doesn't make your feelings any more or less valid. Your feelings are absolutes. They will endure, no matter which word you settle upon.

And here's what you know from those feelings: someone uprooted your life, introducing a new kind of anxiety that you've never felt before. A whole range of horrible emotions that make each day seem unbearable. During the relationship, you may have felt constantly on-edge & unhinged, worried that any mistake could mark the end of your dream. Maybe you found yourself desperately comparing yourself to other people, trying to win back your rightful place by your partner's side.

So I ask you again, does it matter if they were a psychopath?

You already have everything you need to know—from your own feelings. You felt horrible around them, right? So during the relationship, why wasn't that enough to confirm that they should have no place in your life?

Because you were groomed & idealized. You were tricked into falling in love—the strongest of all human bonds—so that your feelings could be more easily manipulated.

Toxic people condition us to ignore our intuition, and you must learn to trust it again. Instead of judging outwardly, perceiving inwardly. When we start focusing on our own feelings, this is where the healing begins. And if you are anything like me, you can agree on this simple truth: good people make you feel good and bad people make you feel bad.

Everything else falls into place from there.

Don't listen to the folks who say your feelings should be totally independent of the world around you. If you've got an open heart, that's impossible. As human beings, we have this incredible gift—the ability to make another person feel wonderful. With a word, a gesture, or a quiet smile. It's what makes the world beautiful. A normal person would probably call this love.

But you experienced an abuser. Someone who manipulated this gift to cause pain. And now you want to know how to avoid them so it'll never happen again. You're worried that you've become hypervigilant—untrusting of everyone and everything around you. You feel that you need a little something extra. Something beyond your intuition.

So this is where I'd like to introduce the idea of a Constant. Your Constant will comfort & protect you throughout this book, and for the rest of your life.

Think of someone you love. Someone who consistently inspires and never disappoints. It could be anyone—your mom, a close friend, a forum member, your children, your cat, a deceased relative. Really, anyone. You might feel that you have no Constant. Of course you do, you just have to dream one up really quick. Imagine a higher power in your mind—one that brings peace to your heart. Colorful, glowing, and full of life. Embodying all of the qualities you admire most: empathy, compassion, kindness. A gentle spirit who will always keep you safe. And viola, you have a Constant.

So now that you've got a Constant in mind (tangible or imagined), I have some questions. Does your Constant make you feel unhinged? Anxious? Jealous? Does your heart rise up into your throat when they speak to you? When you're away from your Constant, do you spend hours analyzing their behavior and defending yourself from hypothetical arguments?

Of course not.

So why is that? Why can one dismissive person make you doubt everything good going on in your life? What's the difference between your Constant and the people who make you feel like garbage?

If you can't answer these questions quite yet, you're not alone. And that's the beauty of it all. You do not need to understand why you don't like being around a person. You have a Constant, and that's all you need to know for now. Self-respect comes later.

Your Constant is a private reminder that you are not crazy, even when it feels like you're taking on the entire world. With time, you will begin to filter out the people who make you feel bad. You realize that you do not need to put up with negativity when there is a Constant who brings out the best in you.

Once you become more comfortable with the idea, you'll be ready to ask the most important question of all: "Shouldn't I feel this same kind of peace with everyone in my life?"

Absolutely. So let's get started.

THE MANUFACTURED
SOUL MATE

Perhaps most insidious of all the psychopath's evils: their
relationship cycle. In which they gleefully and systematically
wipe out the identity of an unsuspecting victim.
Cold & calculated emotional rape.

Personalized Grooming

The psychopath trains you to become the perfect partner.
In a matter of weeks, they take over your entire life, consum-
ing your mind and body with unrivaled pleasure. Ultimately,
you are to become their newest source of endless adoration
and praise—but first, you must fall in love. Then, your heart
will be open to their every suggestion. There are three key
components to this process: idealization, indirect persuasion,
and testing the waters.

Idealization

The idealization phase in a psychopathic relationship will
be unlike anything you've ever experienced. You will be
swept off of your feet, lost in a passionate fantasy with

someone who excites you on every level: emotionally, spiritually, and sexually. They will be the first thing on your mind when you wake up in the morning, waiting for their cheerful, funny texts to start your day. You will quickly find yourself planning a future with them—forgetting about the dull realities of life. None of that matters anymore. They're the person you want to spend the rest of your life with.

While all of this is going on in your heart, their thoughts are occupied by something else entirely: "Good. It's working."

Psychopaths never truly feel the things they display. They're observing you, mirroring your every emotion and pretending to ride this high with you.

Because the higher you rise, the lower you'll fall.

Idealization is the first step in the psychopath's grooming process. Also known as love-bombing, it quickly breaks down your guard, unlocks your heart, and modifies your brain chemicals to become addicted to the pleasure centers firing away. The excessive flattery and compliments play on your deepest vanities and insecurities—qualities you likely don't even know you possess.

They will feed you constant praise & attention through your phone, Facebook timeline, and email inbox. Within a matter of weeks, the two of you will have your own set of inside jokes, pet names, and cute songs. Looking back, you see how insane the whole thing was. But when you're in the middle of it, you can't even imagine life without them.

So how did they do it?

Aside from gifts and poems, the psychopath uses a variety of brainwashing techniques to win you over. They will emphasize six major points during the idealize process:

- **We have so much in common**

We see the world the same way. We have the same sense of humor. We're both so empathetic, constantly helping out our friends & family members. We are perfect for each other.

The psychopath repeatedly drills these points home, often times even going so far as to say: "we're practically the same person." They spend most of the idealize phase listening to you and excitingly responding that they feel the same way. You will eventually come to think that they're the only person you'll ever meet who's so similar to you. And you're right. Because it is flat-out impossible (and creepy) for two people to be identical in every way.

Normal people have differences. It's what makes life interesting. But psychopaths can skip this complication because they don't have an identity. They do not have a sense of self. They don't have life experiences that shape their needs, insecurities, and fantasies. Instead, they steal yours. Like a chameleon, they will transform every part of their personality to become your perfect match.

- **We have the same hopes and dreams**

The psychopath will consume your present life, but they will also take over your future. In order to raise the stakes in the relationship, they will make many long-term promises. This ensures that you are highly invested in the relationship. After all, who wants to stick around for a romance that has no potential future?

The psychopath takes this a step further, quickly discussing major life events like marriage and moving in together. These are decisions that typically take years in a healthy relationship. But you don't need all that time. You already know you'll be spending the rest of your life with them. If you've always dreamed of a family and kids, they will fit that role perfectly. If you want to start a business, they will be your right-hand man/woman. If you're in an unhappy marriage, they will have a plan ready to replace your spouse. You will notice that these plans always seem to involve some sort of sacrifice on your end—never theirs.

• We share the same insecurities

They will never actually say this, of course. But psychopaths can sniff out vulnerabilities in a second. They will mirror your insecurities to drive up your sympathy—so that you attempt to heal their problems with the same care you might hope to receive yourself.

Empathetic people are not attracted to blatant butt-kissing and over confidence. You're attracted to the innocent, sympathetic person. This increases exponentially when you also recognize their insecurities as your own. You see someone feeling inferior, and you believe that you know how to make them feel better.

The psychopath is like no one else, because they genuinely seem to adore all of your efforts. They compares you to past exes, idealizing you above everyone else. It's as if all of your energies finally have a purpose, after likely being frustrated with the unending, not-so-appreciative complaints of others.

If you perceive the psychopath in a sympathetic light, your natural instincts kick in, and you do everything you can to prove how much you care. Psychopaths see insecurities in a very different way—a tool for manipulation and control.

Their childlike "baby" routine is a perfect way to mask these intentions.

- **You are beautiful**

Psychopaths are obsessed with the way you look. You will never meet another human being who comments so frequently on your clothes, your hair, your skin, your pictures, or whatever other superficial quality they choose to focus on that day. At first, these feel like compliments. They can't believe how beautiful or handsome you are—they don't even feel worthy of being your partner. They walk around the park and can't find a person more attractive than you (how this is a compliment, I'm not quite sure).

Going along with the above point about insecurities, you begin to return all of this flattery. You want to make sure they feel adequate—that they understand how attractive you think they are. And that's what they're aiming for. By showering you with compliments, they know they can expect the adoration to rebound shortly. Suddenly, they become very comfortable sharing photos of themselves with you. Your relationship becomes an unending exchange of praise and approval.

You begin to place your self-esteem into their words, because they are so reliably positive. You can actually feel yourself glowing. Your body goes through changes as your confidence rises with their every word. You spend more and more time improving your appearance to keep them impressed.

- **I've never felt this way in my life**

This is where the comparisons begin. They hold you in high regard, far above all of their other relationships. They explain—in detail—every one of the reasons you are better than their exes. They can't remember the last time they've been this happy.

You will constantly hear sweeping declarations like, "I can't believe how lucky I am." Statements like these play on your innate desire to make others happy. They convince you that you're providing them with a special sort of joy, something that they cannot find in anyone else. This becomes a point of pride for you—knowing that you are the one they want, despite all of their other admirers.

The psychopath will refer to you as "perfect" and "flawless", which becomes an overwhelming source of cognitive dissonance when the words inevitably change to "crazy" and "jealous". As you work through these memories, remember that their compliments were always shallow and calculated. They do it with everyone. For each target, the idealize phase will be different. However, one thing remains true throughout each relationship: they really have "never felt this way" in their life. Psychopaths do not actually feel the love and happiness that they so frequently proclaim. They oscillate between contempt, envy, and boredom. Nothing more.

- **We are soul mates**

Psychopaths love the idea of soul mates. It implies something different than love. It says that there are higher powers at work. That you are meant to be together. It means that they consume your entire being—mind and body alike. It creates a psychic bond that lasts long after the relationship has ended.

Perhaps there is a small part in all of us that longs for a soul mate. The perfect person to complete our lives. Someone with whom we can share everything—a lover and a best friend.

And there is nothing wrong with that. I cannot stress this point enough. Psychopaths will manipulate your dreams and fantasies, but that does **not** make them weaknesses. After being discarded by a psychopath, many survivors denounce everything about their past life, raising a permanent guard to protect themselves from more abuse.

Please don't do this.

If you believe in soul mates, you will find a real one. You will meet a man or woman who is full of gentle compassion & kindness. You will never question your heart because of them. Your love will blossom on its own, without all of the manufactured intensity. The psychopath was not your soul mate, and they never will be. To be your soul mate, they would—of course—need to have a soul.

Indirect Persuasion

After they've idealized you, they're ready to begin conditioning your behavior. Using indirect persuasion, psychopaths are able to make subtle suggestions that will ultimately be accepted by their victims. They maintain an illusion of innocence, since most people won't believe "they made me feel these things."

Have you ever noticed how psychopaths always insult their exes as a way to compliment you? Listen closely, they're actually grooming you. By telling you "my ex always used to do this, but you never do", they are **telling** you to behave a certain way. They are falsely flattering a trait that you might not even have. This is not a compliment—it's a warning that if you repeat any of the ex's alleged behavior, you'll be discarded as well. The ex likely didn't even do any of these things. It's just a way for the psychopath to indirectly tell you how they expect you to behave. Here are some of the most common examples:

- "My ex and I always fought. We never fight."
- "My ex always needed to talk on the phone. You're not needy or demanding."
- "My ex would always nag me about getting a job. You're so much more understanding."

Let me say again: these are not compliments. They are expectations. Changes in your perception, to keep them free from inconvenient questions and accusations. To distance you from the truth. They've already come up with a checklist of human emotions that bother them, and now they're planting the idea in your mind: don't express these things, or else.

Normal, empathetic people do not make such comparisons about the people they love. And they certainly don't keep a public tally for everyone involved to see. When you're truly in love, you don't need to convince yourself and others that this experience is better than all of your past experiences. Likewise, if you're falling out of love, you don't need to convince yourself and others that this experience is worse than all of your past experiences.

But psychopaths do this. Every single time. Because it's a strategically ambiguous way to influence your behavior. Now, when you fight, you will try to end it as quickly & pleasantly as possible so you're not like their ex. When you haven't heard from them in three days, you won't call because you don't want to be like their ex. When they're sitting on their rear-end, unemployed for six months, you won't say anything because you don't want to be like their ex.

Any deviation from this plan, and you will receive the silent treatment or a sharp comment about your changed behavior—a reminder that the idealization could end at any time.

This is why most survivors feel so much anger after the abuse has ended. You've been shoving aside your own intuition and needs in order to be "nice". You think you've been giving them some sort of special treatment that no one else can provide. And then suddenly they go running back to the very same people they once used to triangulate you. Meanwhile, you've been repressing the urge to tell them to get a job, or call more often, or just be a good partner. You pushed all of that away because you thought it was the only way to stay with them—to stay on their good side.

Testing the Waters

Once they have you programmed, psychopaths will begin experimenting with their newfound control to see how far they can push you. A useful victim will not talk back to him/her, and they certainly won't defend themselves if the situation calls for it. If the idealize phase worked as planned, you should be more invested in maintaining the passion than standing up for yourself.

During this period, you will see tiny glimpses of the psychopath's darker side. They may teasingly call you a "whore" in the bedroom to see how you react. If you're married, they might casually joke about your spouse's ignorance to the whole situation. They will begin making subtle digs about your intelligence, abilities, and dreams.

These are all tests, and unfortunately if you're reading this book, it means you passed them. If you react in a negative way, the psychopath will assure you that they were obviously joking. As they test the waters, you will begin to feel more and more over-sensitive. You've always considered yourself to be an exceptionally easy-going person, but now you're questioning that. You stop mentioning your concerns, optimistically hoping to keep things perfect.

They use these subtle digs in combination with flattery, ensuring that the addictive brain chemicals continue to fire even when you're feeling upset. This trick slowly trains your mind to ignore your intuition, in favor of the high you feel when you're with them. A psychological reward for submission & servitude.

If you look back at the early stages of your relationship, you will likely remember small warning signs that you chose to ignore. Things that just didn't fit in with the whole "nice guy/girl" persona. Maybe they bragged a little bit too much about how much their ex still wanted them. Or perhaps they "forgot" to call when they promised they would, contacting you hours later than planned. They probably stopped paying for dates, letting you pick up the tab. They blatantly made plans with people that they previously claimed were in love with them. So what did you do? You brushed it all aside. You forgave them quickly and moved forward.

Because you were determined to be different—the partner who could keep them happy and absorb anything, no matter the cost.

And that's when the grooming is complete.

Identity Erosion

The psychopath strips you of your dignity by taking back everything they once pretended to feel during the idealization period. They make a mockery of your dreams, subtly suggesting that you may not be the one for them after all—but nonetheless, stringing you along for the added attention. After grooming you to be dependent & compliant, they use this power to manufacture desperation and desire. In a whirlwind of overwhelming emotions, your fantasy gradually shifts into an inconceivable nightmare.

Destroying Your Boundaries

Like sandpaper, the psychopath will wear away at your self-esteem through a calculated mean-and-sweet cycle. Slowly, your standards will fall so low that you become grateful for the utterly mediocre. Like a frog in boiling water, you won't even realize what happened until it's far too late. Your friends and family will wonder what happened to the man or woman who used to be so strong & energetic. You will frantically excuse their behavior, unable to acknowledge the painful truth behind your relationship: something has changed.

You spend hours waiting by the phone, hoping for that morning text message or a promised phone call. You cancel your plans for the day just to make sure you'll be available for them. You begin to initiate contact more often, brushing aside the nagging sensation that they don't want to talk with you—that they're simply "putting up" with you. You find yourself filling their Facebook wall with compliments and cute jokes, trying to reestablish the perfect dream from the beginning of your relationship. But their responses now feel hollow at best.

You invent romantic stories and exaggerate their positive aspects to anyone who will listen. By convincing others that he or she is a wonderful person, you can continue to live the lie yourself. Throughout the worst of the relationship, your friends and family will likely know them as the "perfect" partner you described. After the relationship ends, it will be confusing and awkward to explain what really happened. Your stories will seem implausible, and your friends will wonder why you didn't speak up sooner. They will not understand that you didn't even know you were in an abusive relationship.

While you're struggling with all of this unexpected anxiety, the psychopath is able to push your boundaries even further. You're in a vulnerable place now, because you're willing to put up with mostly anything—so long as they're paying attention to you.

Their opinions about your appearance become much more critical than before. Suddenly, they begin to notice every little part of your body, commenting freely on your supposed inadequacies. You may even develop an eating disorder, failing to take care of yourself in an effort to keep them interested. Psychopaths are fascinated by body image issues, and will reward your unhealthy habits with the occasional compliment to keep you striving for perfection. Since your self worth is invested entirely in their oscillating opinions, your moods will become conditional and volatile.

They will also begin to humiliate you in front of friends—no longer limited to belittling you behind closed doors. But it will always be done through a guise of humorous intention. You will be hurt to see that others seem to take your partner's side and laugh, despite the way they're making you feel. Psychopaths don't care when they takes a joke too far, and they will dismiss any concerns you might have as hypersensitive. You begin to go along with it, playing the role of a crazy, unintelligent partner whose only purpose is to entertain his or her lover. With time, you will come to believe this façade.

All the while, they will sprinkle intermittent reminders of the idealization phase. If you reach a breaking point, they will always be ready to swoop back in with promises of unlimited love and affection. Although they will never take the blame for their behavior, these superficial distractions will be enough to convince you that they're still the person you fell in love with. And nothing else matters.

Torture by Triangulation

To draw you closer, the psychopath creates an aura of desirability—of being wanted and courted by many. It will become a point of vanity for you to be the preferred object of their attention, to win them away from a crowd of admirers. They manufacture the illusion of popularity by surrounding themselves with members of the opposite sex: friends, former lovers, and your eventual replacement. Then, they create triangles that stimulate rivalry and raise their perceived value. (Adapted from "The Art of Seduction" by Robert Greene).

A note before I continue: people fall in and out of love. People find new love, before and after relationships come to an end. People cheat on one another. This section is not about these everyday occurrences—no matter how heart-breaking and unfair they might be. Instead, I will be describing a very specific set of patterns and behaviors that psychopaths utilize in order to torture and control their targets.

Psychopaths, like most predators, seek power and control. They want to dominate their partners sexually, emotionally, and physically. They do this by exploiting vulnerabilities. This is why they love-bomb you with attention and flattery in the beginning of the relationship—because no matter how strong or confident you are, being in "love" makes you vulnerable by default. Psychopaths don't need physical aggression to control you (although sometimes they do). Instead, relationships provide them with the perfect opportunity to consume you by manufacturing the illusion of love. This is why it's so damaging when bystanders say: "Well, why didn't you just leave?" You never entered a relationship with the psychopath expecting to be abused, belittled, and criticized—first, you were tricked into falling in love, which is the strongest human bond in the world. Psychopaths know this.

So how do psychopaths maintain such a powerful bond over their targets? One of their favorite methods is through triangulation. When I mention this term, survivors usually equate it with the next target, but that is not always the case. Psychopaths use triangulation on a regular basis to seem in "high-demand", and to keep you obsessed with them at all times. This can occur with anyone:

- Your family
- Their family

- Your friends
- Their friends
- Ex-partners
- Partners-to-be
- Complete strangers

The psychopath's ability to groom others is unmatched. They feel an intense euphoria when they turn people against each other, especially when it's over a competition for them. Psychopaths will manufacture situations to make you jealous and question their fidelity. In a normal relationship, people go out of their way to prove that they are trustworthy—but the psychopath does exactly the opposite. They are constantly suggesting that they might be pursuing other options, or spending time with other people, so that you can never settle down into a feeling of peace. And they will always deny this, calling you crazy for bringing it up.

The issue here is that you're accustomed to such a high level of attention after they first lured you in, so it feels very personal & confusing when they direct that attention elsewhere. They know this. They'll "forget" plans with you, and spend a few days with friends that they always complained about to you. They'll ignore you to spend more time with their family, when they initially told you that they were all horrible people. They'll seek sympathy from an ex when a member of their family dies, and explain that they just have a "special friendship" you wouldn't understand. Often—if not always—that ex is someone they first claimed was abusive and unstable.

Seeking attention, sympathy and solace from people who are not **you** is a very common tactic of the psychopath. As an empathetic person, and as their partner, you rightfully feel that they should be seeking comfort in you. You've always healed them in the past, so what's different now? They once claimed that they were a broken person, and that you were the reason they were happy again. But now, they turn to private friendships or past relationships that you could "never understand". And they will always make sure to shove this in your face.

This brings me to the next topic: social media.

Technology makes it so much easier for psychopaths to manipulate through triangulation. It can be as simple as liking a comment from an old ex, while ignoring one from you. They will "accidentally" upload a photo album where they're embracing the ex they once claimed to hate. Everything appears to be unintentional—you often attribute it to insensitivity—but make no mistake: it is carefully calculated.

They will post strategically ambiguous statuses, songs, and videos that suggest you might be "losing" them. They will share things that are intentionally meant to lure in new & old targets. For example, an inside joke with their new victim. Or the love song that they once shared with their ex. This does two things: it leaves you feeling unhinged, anxious, and jealous. But it also makes the competing party feel confident, loved, and special. They are grooming others as they erode your identity—two birds with one stone.

They want you to confront them about these things, because they are so seemingly minimal that you will appear crazy and jealous for bringing it up. They will calmly provide an excuse for everything and then blame you. Covert abuse is impossible to prove, because it's always strategically ambiguous. You can't prove that they're luring in their ex because of a song they posted, but you know it intuitively. This is how they finalize the crazy-making. Because let's be honest: complaining about Facebook statuses & comments does seem immature. That's exactly how they want you to feel.

Psychopaths are also expertly skilled at surrounding themselves with givers—insecure people who find self-worth in taking care of others. This is why your giving seems so insignificant and replaceable during the relationship. They adore qualities in others who are nothing like you—sometimes even the exact opposite of you. The message is simple: you are no longer special. You are replaceable. If you don't give them the worshipping they deserve, they'll always have other sources. And even if you do give them positive energy, they'll get bored of you eventually. They don't need you. Their current round of fans will always spoil and admire them, making you believe that they truly must be a great person. But take a careful look around. You'll notice that they all seem to have an unspoken misery about them.

The final triangulation happens when they make the decision to abandon you. This is when they'll begin freely talking about how much this relationship is hurting them, and how they don't know if they can deal with your behavior anymore. They will usually mention talking to a close friend about your relationship, going into details about how they both agreed that your relationship wasn't healthy. In the meantime, they've been blatantly ignoring frantic messages from you. You'll be sitting there wondering why they aren't chatting with you about these concerns, considering it's **your** relationship.

Well, the reason is that they've already made the decision to dump you—now they're just torturing you. They only seek advice from people they know will agree with them. That "friend" they're talking to is probably their next target.

After the breakup, they will openly brag about how happy they are with their new partner, where most normal people would feel very embarrassed and secretive about entering a new relationship so quickly. And even more surprising, they fully expect you to be happy for them. Otherwise you are bitter and jealous.

During this period, they make a post-dump assessment. If you grovel or beg, they are likely to find some value in your energy. They will be both disgusted and delighted by your behavior. If you lash out and begin uncovering their lies, they will do everything in their power to drive you to suicide. Even if you come back to them later with an apology, they will permanently despise any target who once dared talk back to them. You've seen too much—the predator behind the mask.

This is why they constantly wave their new partner in your face, posting pictures and declaring their happiness online. Proving how happy and perfect they are. It's a final attempt to drive you insane with triangulation. To make you blame the new target, instead of the true abuser.

Exes who stay strung do not understand that they are puppets to the psychopath. Instead, they feel that they are fulfilling some sort of beautiful duty as a friend—someone who will always be there for them. They don't understand that they are only kept around to spice things up when the psychopath becomes bored. They don't see that they are the basis of so many fights—not because their friendship with the psychopath is special and enviable, but because the psychopath intentionally creates that drama. They are operating under the delusion that their friendship with the psychopath is brilliant, unique, and unprecedented. When in reality, they are just used for triangulation.

So how can you protect yourself from this devastating emotional abuse? First, you must learn self-respect. I will discuss this in more detail later on in the book. But the bottom line is, you need know what is acceptable and unacceptable behavior in a relationship. You should know that a partner who cheats and antagonizes is not worth your time. You should never resort to calling yourself crazy in order to account for their extremely sketchy behavior. But that's hard to do with subtle, covert, crazy-making abuse.

So here's where I introduce "The Detective Rule". The idea is simple: if you find yourself playing detective with someone, you remove them from your life immediately. Remember your Constant? Do you play detective with them? Do you cyberstalk their Facebook page and question their every intention? No, of course not. So you know the common denominator is external.

Even if this sense of distrust feels obscure and unreasonable, trust your gut. If you are constantly worrying or doubting your thoughts, it's time to stop blaming yourself and start taking action.

Miraculously, every single time you remove that toxic person from your life, you will find that the anxiety subsides. Some of us are better at judging ourselves than others, so this finally gives you a chance to put that to use. You can decide whether or not you like the way you feel around someone. No one can ever tell you that your feelings are wrong. Remember the question: "How are you feeling today?" The answer is all that matters.

Triangulation leaves long-lasting emotional scars, and it makes you feel as if you are a jealous, needy, insecure monster. Start healing those scars and understand that they were manufactured. You were not yourself—you were manipulated. The real you is kind, loving, open-minded, and compassionate. Never question these things again.

Manufactured Emotions

During a relationship with a psychopath, you are likely to experience a range of emotions that you've never felt before: extreme jealousy, neediness, rage, anxiety, and paranoia. After every outburst, you constantly think to yourself, "If only I hadn't behaved that way, then maybe they'd be happier with me."

Think again.

Those were not your emotions. I repeat: those were not your emotions. They were carefully manufactured by the psychopath in order to make you question your own good nature. Victims are often of the mentality that they can forgive, understand and absorb all of the problems in a relationship. Essentially, they checkmate themselves by constantly trying to rationalize the abuser's completely irrational behavior.

For example, you probably didn't consider yourself to be a jealous person before you met the psychopath. You might have even taken pride in being remarkably relaxed and open-minded. The psychopath recognizes this and seeks to exploit it. During the grooming phase, they draw you in by flattering those traits—they just can't believe how perfect you are. The two of you never fight. There's never any drama. You're so easy-going compared to their crazy, evil ex.

But behind the scenes, something else is going on. Psychopaths become bored very easily, and the idealization is only fun until they have you hooked. Once that happens, these strengths of yours become vulnerabilities that they use against you. They begin to inject as much drama into the relationship as they possibly can, throwing you into impossible situations and then judging you for reacting to them.

Most people would agree that jealousy is toxic in a relationship. But there's a huge difference between true jealousy and the psychopath's manufactured jealousy.

Take the following two (exaggerated) conversations:

Case 1:

<u>Boyfriend</u>: Hey, my old high-school friend is coming into town if you'd like to meet her!

<u>Girlfriend</u>: No! Why do you need other female friends? You have me.

In this case, the girlfriend truly seems to have some jealousy issues that need to be addressed. Assuming the boyfriend hasn't abused her in the past, this is an inappropriate display of jealousy.

Case 2:

<u>Boyfriend</u>: My ex is coming into town. You know, the crazy abusive one who's still completely obsessed with me.

<u>Girlfriend</u>: Oh, I'm sorry to hear that!

<u>Boyfriend</u>: We're probably going to meet up later for drinks. She always hits on me when she drinks.

<u>Girlfriend</u>: I'm confused. Could we talk about this in person?

<u>Boyfriend</u>: You have a problem with it?

<u>Girlfriend</u>: Nope! No problem. I guess I was just a little confused since you said she abused you. But I hope things go well! It's nice when exes are able to be friends.

<u>Boyfriend</u>: Jesus Christ, you're so jealous sometimes.

<u>Girlfriend</u>: I'm sorry, I'm not trying to be jealous. I was just confused at first.

<u>Boyfriend</u>: Your jealousy is ruining our relationship and

creating so much unnecessary drama.

<u>Girlfriend</u>: I'm sorry! We don't have to talk about it in person. I really didn't mean to come across that way.

<u>Boyfriend</u>: It's fine, I forgive you. We'll just have to work through your jealousy issues.

In this case, the psychopath did three things:

- Put you in an impossible situation that would make any human being jealous, especially after talking about how much their ex loves them.
- Accused you of being jealous, even though you tried to respond reasonably.
- Played "good cop" by offering to forgive you for a problem that they created in the first place. This places them in their favorite role of teacher vs. student.

The longer this abuse occurs, the more you begin to wonder if you actually have a jealousy problem.

And it's not just limited to jealousy. To offer another example, you may have begun to feel needy and clingy during the relationships with the psychopath. But again, it's all manufactured. Who was the one responsible for initiating constant conversation and attention in the first place? It was them. Once they're bored, they will start to lash out at you for trying to continue practices that they initiated.

Again, most people would agree that neediness is toxic in a relationship. But there's a huge difference between true neediness and the psychopath's manufactured neediness.

Case 1:

<u>Girlfriend</u>: Hey, I won't be around tonight because my

grandmother wants to get dinner. Sorry!
Boyfriend: Oh my god, I haven't seen you in three hours.
This is getting ridiculous. You better text me the entire
time.

In this case, the boyfriend truly seems to have some neediness issues that need to be addressed. Assuming the girlfriend hasn't abused him in the past, this is an inappropriate
display of neediness.

Case 2:
Boyfriend: Hi, I haven't heard from you in three days.
Just want to make sure you're doing okay.
Girlfriend: Jesus, I have a life outside of you, you know.
Boyfriend: I know, I was just sort of confused because
I'm used to hearing from you each morning.
Girlfriend: You're so needy. I have important things to do
and I can't just drop everything to text you.
Boyfriend: I'm sorry, I didn't mean to sound needy. It was
the first text I've sent in three days.
Girlfriend: I can't deal with this. I've never met someone
so needy in my life.
Boyfriend: I'm really sorry! I won't bother you again.
Girlfriend: It's fine, I forgive you. We'll just have to work
through your neediness issues.

Once again, the psychopath did three things:

* Put you in an impossible situation that would make
  any human being needy, especially after the constant
  attention in the idealize phase.

- Accused you of being needy, even though you tried to respond reasonably.
- Played "good cop" by offering to forgive you for a problem that they created in the first place. This places them in their favorite role of teacher vs. student.

The longer this abuse occurs, the more you begin to wonder if you're actually a needy person. I could go on like this for paranoia, anger, hysteria—and every other nasty emotion you felt around them.

You must understand that in loving, healthy relationships, no one would ever put you in these situations in the first place. Your boundaries were put to the test, and you did the absolute best you could, given the circumstances. In the future, you should never allow someone to tell you who you are or how you feel.

Putting You on the Defense

If you're dealing with a psychopath, it's a given that they will make unfounded accusations about you at some point— especially if you're starting to put together the red flags in their behavior. These insults have a very specific purpose: to put you on the defense.

Why?

It's actually a lot simpler than you might think. People who defend themselves seem guilty by default. Whether or not they deserve it, that's the unfortunate truth about how most people think. We've seen lives destroyed because of this phenomenon—a man falsely accused of rape, destroying his reputation even after he's proven innocent. It doesn't matter. No one trusts him anymore.

So the psychopath says all sorts of ridiculous things, and you're suddenly defending yourself from accusations you've never even dreamed of. How could you not? Your name is being smeared—if not to others, then to the partner who supposedly loves you. So you get caught up in trying to prove them wrong, and that's where the calculated self-destruction begins.

The psychopath can sit back, relax, and enjoy the show. They can calmly point to the hysterical victim and say "Jeeze, that poor, crazy person…" Essentially, they provoke your anger, and then calmly use it to prove their own point.

Nobody likes negativity, especially when that negativity is directed at someone they like. When you feel the need to expose a psychopath's lies, you'll find yourself saying a lot of negative things. "They're the liar, here's the proof!" or "They cheated on me, here's the proof!" or "They've done the same thing with ten other partners, here's the proof!". The problem is, nobody cares about the proof. They just see obsession and jealousy, as the psychopath will groom them to believe.

Because you're defending yourself, you seem like the guilty one. They're just on the sidelines, playing innocent after provoking you. And again, you can never convince anyone of that.

Here's the most important thing to remember: defending yourself will only make things worse. Sometimes less is more, and this is one of those times. You think you have a perfect response to their ridiculous defamation? Yes, the psychopath is counting on that. In fact, they've carefully crafted their insults to make sure of it. They attack the things you value most, because those are the things in life you will defend most passionately.

And make no mistake—it's intentional.

The easiest way for them to suck you in is to accuse you of doing things that they themselves did. It's almost too easy for you to point out the hypocrisy. And that's the point—yes, it's too easy. Because it's a trap. If you have a perfect retort to their garbage, there's a reason for that. Do not fall for it. They want you on the defense, trying to prove yourself to everyone, including them. Once you've taken the bait, their job is done.

Word Salad

When they're feeling threatened or bored, psychopaths will often use what's called "word salad" in an attempt to keep your mind occupied. Basically, it's a conversation from hell. They aren't actually saying anything at all. They're just talking at you. Before you can even respond to one outrageous statement, they're already on to the next. You'll be left with your head spinning. Study the warning signs, and disengage before any damage can be done:

- **Circular conversations**

You'll think you worked something out, only to begin discussing it again in two minutes. And it's as if you never even said a word the first time around. They begin reciting all of the same tired garbage, ignoring any legitimate arguments you may have provided moments ago. If something is going to be resolved, it will be on their terms. With psychopaths, the same issues will come up over and over again—why are they so friendly with their ex again? Why are they suddenly not paying any attention to you? Why do they sound so eager to get off the phone? And every time you bring up these issues, it's as if you never even had the argument in the past. You get sucked back in, only to feel crazy & high-maintenance when they decide "I'm sick of always arguing about this." It's a merry-go-round.

- **Bringing up your past wrongdoings & ignoring their own**

If you point out something nasty they're doing—like ignoring you or cheating—they'll mention something totally unrelated from the past that you've done wrong. Did you used to drink too much? Well then, their cheating isn't really all that bad compared to your drinking problem. Were you late to your first date two years ago? Well then, you can't complain about them ignoring you for three days straight. And God forbid you bring up any of their wrongdoings. Then, you are a bitter lunatic with a list of grievances.

- **Condescending & patronizing tone**

The entire conversation will have this calm, cool demeanor. It's almost as if they're mocking you, gauging your reactions to see how much further they can push. When you finally react emotionally, that's when they'll tell you to calm down, raise their eyebrows, smirk, or feign disappointment. The whole point of word salad is to make you unhinged, and therefore give them the upper hand. Because remember, conversations are competitions—just like anything else with a psychopath.

- **Accusing you of doing things that they themselves are doing**

I mentioned this in the previous section about psychopaths putting you on the defense. In heated arguments, psychopaths have no shame. They will begin labeling you with their own horrible qualities. It goes beyond projection, because most people project unknowingly. Psychopaths know they are smearing you with their own flaws, and they are seeking a reaction. After all, how can you not react to such blatant hypocrisy?

- **Multiple personas**

Through the course of a word salad conversation, you're likely to experience a variety of their personalities. It's sort of like good cop, bad cop, demented cop, stalker cop, scary cop, baby cop. If you're pulling away, sick of their abuse and lies, they will restore a glimpse of the idealize phase. A little torture to lure you back in with empty promises. If that doesn't work, suddenly they'll start insulting the things they once idealized. You'll be left wondering who you're even talking to, because their personas are imploding as they struggle to regain control. Our beloved administrator, Victoria, summed this up perfectly: "The devil itself was unleashed in a desperate fit of fury after being recognized: twisting, turning, writhing, spewing, flattering, sparkling, vomiting."

- **The eternal victim**

Somehow their cheating and lying will always lead back to a conversation about their abusive past or a crazy ex. You will end up feeling bad for them, even when **they've** done something horribly wrong. You will instead use it as an opportunity to bond with them over their supposed complex feelings. And once they have successfully diverted your attention elsewhere, everything will go back to the way it was. No bonding or deep spiritual connection whatsoever. Psychopaths cry "abuse"—but in the end, you are the one left with nothing.

• **You begin explaining basic human emotions**

You find yourself explaining things like "empathy" and "feelings" and "being nice". Normal adults do not need to be taught the golden rules from kindergarten. You are not the first person who has attempted to see the good in them, and you will not be the last. You think to yourself, "if they can just understand why I'm hurt, then they'll stop doing it." But they won't. They wouldn't have done it in the first place if they were a decent human being. The worst part is, they pretended to be decent when you first met—sucking you in with this sweet, caring persona. They know how to be kind & good, but they find it boring.

• **Excuses**

Everyone messes up every now and then, but psychopaths recite excuses more often than they actually follow through with promises. Their actions never match up with their words. You are disappointed so frequently that you feel relieved when they do something decent—they condition you to become grateful for the mediocre.

- **"What in the world just happened"**

These conversations leave you drained. You will be left with an actual headache. You will spend hours, even days, obsessing over the argument. You'll feel as if you exhausted all of your emotional energy to accomplish absolutely nothing. You will have a million pre-planned arguments in your head, ready to respond to all the unaddressed points that you couldn't keep up with. You will feel the need to defend yourself. You'll try to come up with a diplomatic solution that evenly distributes the blame, and therefore gives you both a chance to apologize and make up. But in the end, you'll find that you're the only one apologizing.

The Transitional Target

This section comes directly from a conversation I had with a dear friend, so it may feel a bit personal at times. I've done my best to edit it to apply to a broader audience. It's a special note for anyone who felt unusually disposable compared to their other targets. It will also apply to survivors who were in long-term relationships with psychopaths, as many of them were trapped with families & children.

Psychopaths are always on the prowl, you know this. But after a longer, more "substantial" relationship, they are usually seeking to take out their hatred and contempt on one poison container (a phrase coined by Kelli from TheAbilityToLove)—a temporary target to dispose of as soon as they find something else. Because of this, you tend to get ripped out of the idealize phase much faster than most. Additionally, the idealize phase is lazy: no money, no actions, no real treatment. Just words. You got a lot of words, which sucked you in, because you wanted to believe the words so badly.

But as the psychopath transitions from two "stable" relationships, they need something to fill the void in between. Although they likely don't even have the next target scouted out yet, they already know they're not staying with you. But to you, the relationship means everything—it's attention and appreciation you've never experienced before. It appeals to your deepest dreams of making someone else happy, after all of their alleged pain and sadness. It seems like they know you so well. You finally found a soul mate after so much loneliness and frustration.

But, as you're starting to see, their actions never match up with their words. Psychopaths are especially indifferent with transitional targets, not really caring one way or another—leaving you with the feeling that they're being insensitive. You tend to fill in their abuse with your own love, in hopes that you can restore the brief idealize phase. Targets often experience cognitive dissonance, trying to project their own reasoning onto an unreasonable person. But their behavior is neither accidental nor unintentional.

And then comes the most heartbreaking moment: they discard you and go running off with another person who they suddenly seem ready to settle down with. They move in together, post pictures, pay for things, and live the life you always dreamed of. It's the ultimate insult when you were not given any of that special treatment. Basically, as soon as they got their quick fix of power & control over you, they felt re-energized and ready to scout out their next great adventure.

Statistically, most victims return to their abusers seven times before they finally realize the treatment is unacceptable and leave for good. So here is the cycle these victims are left with, with each idealize & devalue getting progressively worse:

- Idealize, devalue, idealize, devalue, idealize, devalue (repeat) → Finally a breaking point

This is what transitional targets get:

- Mediocre idealize phase with huge promises that make you feel amazing → Sudden discard out of no-where.

This leaves you with zero closure because you can't even look back at the cycle of violence that exists for most people. Not that you would want to by any means, but you're basically just left in limbo after the abandonment. From such a ridiculous high to a devastating low, with no time or perspective to realize what just happened. It's emotional torture. You are left only with an intense love and a horrible discard.

Psychopaths use their mind games on every target—it's always the same. The difference is, transitional targets never experience that "full" idealize phase, with some time and stability for things to blow up. This is because the psychopath never intended for the transitional target to become a stable part of their life to begin with. You were perfect for what they wanted at the time: attention and admiration.

But they also recognized that you were emotionally intelligent and uniquely perceptive. The fact that you're reading this book is not some sort of accident—you're a truth seeker, determined to find out what just happened to you.

For others, the highs and the lows are less extreme, which is useful but also ironically frustrating to the psychopath.

Psychopaths settle for targets who don't truly see their nasty behavior. If you're reading this now, that means the psychopath could never settle for you, because over the course of months, years, or decades, you saw through the facade. They need someone who won't catch on. Ever.

So yes, on one hand, the eventual long-term victim is useful, because they won't point out their lying and cheating. But on the other hand, the psychopath silently resents these people for not seeing through their facade. Strange, right? They pretend to give off this perfect, happy image with their "settlement", but they much prefer the thrill of someone more empathetic—someone who truly feels the torture of their mind games. But the psychopath can rarely have one of these people permanently, so instead he or she uses them during transition periods, like a quick high before the settlement.

Every once in a while, though, they will end up spending years with a highly empathetic person. I know several of these people from the forum, usually locked in by family or children. These dynamics often seem to result in horrific discards and physical abuse, because over time, the target forms a remarkable understanding of their abuser.

Many survivors tell stories of love-bombing that lacked the actual courtship seen with their next target or previous ex. You never got to spend as much time with them as the others, right? Instead, you experienced a much shorter fling, cut off abruptly in the middle of the idealize phase with some unbelievably vicious identity erosion. And then suddenly they've settled down with another partner, leaving you wondering how they're able to spend years with that person, when they could barely handle a few months with you.

And that's the point—psychopaths typically can't last long with empathetic people (except for cases with children & long-term manipulation), because you tend to absorb their poison. Yes, they get the high of sweeping you off your feet and making you a perfect servant to their mind games. But the downside is, eventually you subconsciously spit that poison right back in their face. You don't want to ruin the idealize phase, but you find yourself unable to stop pointing out their lies and changed behavior.

Transitional targets & truth-seeking targets (anyone reading this book) figured them out, all the way down to their nasty core. Psychopaths would never admit it, but they'll always have a bitter respect for people who can see them for what they really are. And at the same time, they'll also strongly resent those who can't—even though that's all they can get in the long run. This is why they always lose and feel a need to reinvent the rules of the game, to convince themselves that their choice is correct.

But the fact is, psychopaths settle. They always do. And that's why they needed to destroy you before settling. To convince themselves that they're not losing anything special. So why not make you self-destruct—even kill yourself. Perfect, the nagging doubts are finally gone.

And from your perspective, this is why you're left so resentful and angry. You did so much, encouraged by their fake appreciation that kept you going. At the very least, why couldn't they be a jerk from the start so you'd know not to waste your time and emotions? Instead, they used words and chemicals to brainwash you into giving, giving, and more giving. So when they not only don't appreciate it—but actually destroy you—you're left feeling broken and empty. It's not human. And then you see them running off with someone else, paying for things, settling down a bit... It makes you think "Hey, maybe they are capable of a relationship after all. Maybe the problem was me."

No, the problem was not you. And it never will be.

Sexual Manipulation

Sex with the psychopath seemed perfect at first. They knew exactly where to touch you, what to say, and when to do the right things. You were perfectly compatible in the bedroom, right?

Well, sort of.

Like everything else, the psychopath also mirrored your deepest sexual desires. That's why it felt so incredibly passionate and flawless when you were together—and that's why it feels like rape during the identity erosion. Because the psychopath does not, in fact, share your most intimate fantasies. Instead, they've been observing and tailoring their behavior to match yours. It's shocking when you realize this, because you come to understand that they never felt the emotional and spiritual pleasure that you felt. While you were at your most vulnerable, they were simply watching & learning.

You find yourself in a desperate situation, needing their sexual approval and flattery to feel attractive. They use this to control their targets. They pull away in order to make you seem desperate, needy, and slutty. In the idealize phase, they couldn't get enough of you. But once they have you hooked, they begin to play mind games. They withhold sex, redefining it as a privilege that they hold the key to.

When you're lying next to them in bed, you can practically feel them waiting for you to make the next move. They're ready to mock you—to make you feel unnatural and sex-crazed. They will laugh at you, insulting you with jokes that aren't even remotely funny. The passionate sex you remember has been replaced by a game. A competition.

They will make you feel ugly by announcing that their sex drive is lower than ever—that they haven't even had sexual thoughts in weeks. The implication is clear: they haven't thought about **you** in weeks.

And then, when the triangulation begins, you find it impossible to believe that they could have such a great sex life with anyone else. How could they? You seemed like physical soul mates. They liked all of the same things as you. But remember, it was manufactured. If you loved something in the bedroom, the psychopath quickly picked up on that in the grooming phase. They'll pick up on something else entirely for their next victim.

Sex with a psychopath is no different than rape. You unknowingly formed a chemical bond with a con artist. Your consent was based on a lie. So many survivors blame themselves because they couldn't get past the sexual addition, keeping them bonded to their abuser. But it's not your fault. You were tricked into feeling an overwhelmingly strong attachment during the grooming phase. And then they manipulated that—toying with the toxic addiction firing through your body.

You will reclaim your sexual freedom, and that is a promise. We have an open and honest dialog about sex at PsychopathFree.com. It is a hugely important part of the psychopathic relationship cycle, and more importantly—it plays an essential role in your own healing process. Recovery is a joint effort of the mind and body.

Gaslighting & Projection

The psychopath's crazy-making behavior will ultimately make you question your own sanity. Isolated from your support network, your understanding of reality will start to slip. Given enough time, you will begin to absorb the very core of their being—a lingering evil that you've never felt before. The dark void of their soul.

Psychopaths can neither feel nor understand the phenomenon of unconditional love, so they decide it doesn't exist. And because they are eternally jealous & manipulative, they assume everyone else operates the same way. The longer you spend with a psychopath, the more you will begin to question your own good nature.

Our invaluable administrator, Smitten Kitten, explains this mind-boggling process clearly & coherently:

"Psychopaths project and blame you for their own behavior. They accuse you of being negative when they are the most negative people in the world. They gaslight you into believing that your normal reactions to their abuse are the problem—not the abuse itself. When you feel angry and hurt because of their silent treatment, broken promises, lying, or cheating, there is something wrong with **you**. When you call them out on their dishonest behavior, you're the abnormal one who is too sensitive, too critical, and always focusing on the negative.

This is all part of the brainwashing process. Acting inappropriately, unacceptably, downright abusively—and then trying to turn it around to make it your fault. Adding insult to injury. They intentionally cause pain you don't deserve, all the while denying they've done anything to begin with. And on top of that, they try to make it **your** fault—so that you blame yourself for something that supposedly didn't even happen.

Yes, re-read that. That's how illogical it is.

It's their parting "gift" to dump all of the blame on you for the looming failure of the relationship. Problem is, it never even had a chance to begin with.

If only you had maintained the glowing optimism and naivety you felt during the love-bombing stage—throughout all of their subsequent lies and abuse. Then everything would have been fine. If only you hadn't questioned the contradictions and lies you recalled from letters that they later denied sending. Yes, if only you had stayed compliant and quiet, in spite of the overwhelming evidence staring you in the face— evidence they planted, just to test you. Then it would all be fine.

But even then, they would become bored and disappointed that you hadn't caught on or challenged them. So they'd invent something to accuse you of, in order to justify their abuse and create drama. No matter what you do, it's always a lose-lose situation with a psychopath. They want you to believe you're the loser when really, it's them."

Silence

The silent treatment is a brutal form of abuse—one that pins you against your own mind. You declare war on your intuition and everything that you know to be true. Once your identity has been sufficiently eroded, the psychopath can use this final technique without any chance that you'll leave them. Instead, you will torture yourself, carrying out the remainder of the abuse for them.

They will leave you alone with your thoughts, planting subtle hints and suggestions over social networking to encourage your paranoia. You will run through everything you've done in the relationship, blaming yourself for your feelings & emotions. You will wake up in the middle of the night, heart racing as you hope for a text from them. Nothing. You log into Facebook and see them chatting away with friends and exes. They're not unavailable—they're ignoring you.

You will be expected to understand that they cannot talk for days on end, despite texting you on an hourly basis in the beginning of the relationship. You will begin to feel that you are on "probation", despite having no idea what you've done wrong. You may become passive aggressive, drafting out long emails about their changed behavior and complete lack of contact. You might even feel strongly enough to suggest a break, but you will never follow through with it for more than a few hours. You will think you can out-ignore them, remaining calm and collected like nothing is wrong. But they will always win this game. Because they do not need your attention—they have already found someone else.

Yes, when the psychopath begins ignoring you for days, it means they've found a new target. Otherwise, they would continue focusing all of their efforts on you. But now, you are just an obstacle. They've found something new and exciting—your emotions are just a bothersome speed bump in their latest romantic venture. They will never tell you this. They will just continue to read your desperate text messages, ignoring them without another word. They will lash out and accuse you of being obnoxious, crazy, and clingy. They will refuse to discuss anything over the phone or in person, unless it happens entirely on their terms. The abuse is no longer covert. Their contempt for you is unmistakable.

But despite all of this, they will not dump you. Not yet. They're saving that for the right moment.

The Grand Finale

The psychopath carefully selects the most indifferent & heartbreaking way imaginable to abandon you. They want you to self-destruct, cleaning up any loose ends as they begin the grooming process with their latest victim. They destroy you as a way to reassure themselves that their new target is better. But most importantly, they destroy you because they hate you. They despise your empathy & love—qualities they must pretend to feel every single day. To destroy you is to temporarily silence the nagging reminder of the emptiness that consumes their soul.

Setup

The discard will feel casual and impulsive, but make no mistake—it has been planned for weeks, if not months. During this process, you will begin to feel that they actually **want** you to dump them. They will go out of their way to upset & harm you, and you will know in your heart that they have no interest in continuing the relationship. But again, they will never say this. They will deny any suggestions you might have about their intentions. Instead, they will unload all of the blame on you, making you feel that your self-destructive behavior is what's really ruining the relationship—not their blatant abuse tactics.

While you're frantically running around trying to fix things, they will be courting their next target. They may already be sleeping together. They use your increasingly volatile behavior as a pity ploy for their current victim. What better way to convince them of your insanity than to present them with your seemingly unprovoked & hysterical text messages?

You will spend all of this time thinking that they've just lost interest, or that your jealousy issues extinguished the spark. Months into recovery, things will finally start to click. You will be able to look back at the pre-breakup performance and put all of the pieces into place. You will be shocked—unable to comprehend such a cunning scheme. You will be disgusted when you realize how long you were strung along. You will wonder why they didn't just dump you the moment they met someone new. You will realize that they were blatantly ignoring you—not because they were busy with work—but because they were busy in bed.

And all the while, they made **you** feel like the monster.

The Talk

When the psychopath breaks up with you, it will feel nonchalant and disingenuous. They might even do it over a text-message to make you feel completely worthless. They will talk mostly about themselves and their "feelings"— explaining that they just can't go on like this anymore. You will remain paralyzed and numb throughout the conversation. You knew it was coming, but you just can't believe it happened. You will hear a lot of word salad about their ex and your changed behavior, but nothing about the target they're replacing you with. They will appear both pitiful (of you) and oddly cheerful.

They will choose the most inconvenient setting possible in which to dump you. If you live cross-country, they will have no problem letting you come out to visit them, only to dump you halfway through the trip. By disrupting your travel plans and removing you from familiar surroundings, they ensure that you will be completely unhinged for the news—adding to the confusion and inferiority that you already feel.

You will leave the breakup feeling nothing but emptiness. I cannot describe this feeling as depression, because it is worse than that. In this moment, you will feel that your spirit has died.

Triangulation Again

The psychopath isn't done with you yet. Their favorite time to triangulate is right after the breakup. After they change their relationship status to "Single" on Facebook, you will think that things can't possibly get any worse. You have friends asking how you're doing, but you're not able to focus on anything except your ex partner. Looking at their pictures makes you feel sick, but you keep doing it anyway. You scroll through old memories, impulsively deleting what you can—immediately regretting it afterwards.

And then you see it.

A few days after the breakup, they're posting pictures with someone else. Someone you've never seen before. They make no effort to hide their latest conquest. In fact, it feels like they're showing the new target off. They feel no embarrassment and no guilt. You know it's a bad idea, but your curiosity gets the best of you. You start peeking around, discovering that this new person has been interacting with your ex for a while now. They've been joking around and subtly flirting, but you never noticed. You were probably completely focused on the ex before you.

Before you know it, they've changed their relationship status and their friends are all enthusiastically congratulating the happy couple. They've clearly known about the new partner for some time now. While you were written off as the crazy ex, the next target was already preparing to take your place. The psychopath's fan club cheers for them, clapping louder than ever before—their hero has found the (latest) love of his or her life.

Superiority Complex

After the breakup & triangulation, psychopaths feel an immense amount of superiority. This is when they're at their best—glowing with energy as they watch you fall from grace. It's what they live for. They put their newest target on display because they want you to know about him/her. They're waiting for your reaction. And if you don't react, they will invent a reason to talk to you, making sure their new profile picture is displayed front and center. Often times, psychopaths will use pointless requests as an excuse to get your attention. For example, returning an article of clothing or a DVD. Something that any normal person would just forget about.

Once they have your attention, they will adopt a calm, patronizing demeanor. Talking down to you as if they're somehow the relationship guru because they're happy and you're single. The whole conversation will take on a very arrogant, "I'm-in-charge" sort of attitude. After the breakup, they're obsessed with being the calm & superior person. The winner.

They will minimize everything that happened, warning you not to create any drama. Instead of apologizing for their abusive behavior and now-obvious cheating, they make sweeping statements explaining that breakups are just difficult. They depersonalize the experience and speak down to you as if they pity you. They use this pseudo-pleasantry to come across as the bigger person. They will wish you all the best, playing it off casually. Ending things on their terms. They will make it seem as if this was just an everyday breakup.

If you don't allow them the post-breakup superiority routine, they will become extremely unpleasant. They do not want to talk about their infidelity or lies. They want you to idolize them in your memory. And remember how they gave you the silent treatment for days at the end of your relationship? Well, they still expect prompt responses from you—otherwise you're bitter & jealous.

If you feel like punching a wall by this point, you're in good company.

Backwards

In most cases, psychopaths are obsessed with making sure that they break up with you. This is a sign of power & control. But there are occasions when a survivor finally breaks free on their own, leaving the psychopath and liberating themselves from the abuse.

When the psychopath is the one who's discarded, you should prepare yourself for months—if not years—of stalking and harassment. Until they find another victim, they will pour all of their rage into ruining your life through intimidation and scare tactics. They will invent online personas to cyberstalk your internet activity. This gives them the illusion of control—reassurance that you cannot exist without them.

They may also try to win you back. Don't be fooled. This is their final manipulative attempt to turn the tables—so that the dumping can occur on their terms. It sounds ridiculous that someone would go through the trouble of courting you just to dump you, but this is how psychopaths work.

Survivors often wish that their ex would make some form of contact, just for the validation that they haven't been forgotten. But you are the lucky one. If you need any further confirmation of this, speak to someone who dumped a psychopath. You will hear their stories and quickly understand that your ex's silence is a wonderful gift.

The Irony

Strangely enough, the grand finale is also the psychopath's greatest tribute to your strength. It reveals their accidental respect for you. It seems impossible, because you're at rock bottom. You've never felt so worthless in your life. And this is exactly how the psychopath wants you to feel. But why?

There are four general cases that result in a grand finale. And in every single one of them, the psychopath is giving you an indirect compliment:

- **They've found another partner**

If the psychopath sees their new target as more valuable than you, what exactly does that say? It means that he or she is more likely to provide them with the unconditional adoration that they crave. It also means you're not doing enough of that. When the psychopath dumps you for another target, they are writing you off as a less useful victim. They see you as less submissive, less controllable, and less vulnerable than their new target. When they dump you and rub the other partner in your face, they're not proving how happy they are. They're trying to erode your self-esteem so that they can convince themselves that you're worse than their new conquest.

The only time people need to prove their happiness to others is when they are, in fact, unhappy. When psychopaths triangulate you and post new pictures for the world to see, they're not happy. They're miserably and pathetically trying to convince themselves of a lie by manufacturing your downfall. They're complimenting you in their obsession with your failure.

• You caught up with their lies

Did you ever hear this phrase: "God, you over-analyze everything"? Strange how your supposed over-analyzing was always a result of their cheating, lying, and triangulating. That phrase is the psychopath's way of making you feel crazy for pointing out the truth. When they punish you for pointing out their lies, they are once again complimenting you. By trying to destroy your sanity and intuition, they are telling you that these qualities of yours are currently too strong. They recognize these traits and try to convince you that they are weaknesses—ensuring that you won't use them anymore. If a psychopath accuses you of over-analyzing everything, it just means you're a good detective.

• **You're too happy**

Psychopaths love to build people up in the idealize phase, but then resent the happiness & love generated by their partners. Weird, right? It makes absolutely no sense. So the psychopath's solution is to harbor this resentment through passive-aggressive abuse. They make you feel unhinged & anxious, shattering all of the confidence that **they** built up. When they do this, they are flattering you. This means you embodied everything they hate: love, happiness & joy. They despise these qualities, because it's a reminder of everything they can never feel. Qualities they see as stupid and useless. Your smiles and laughter are a strange, nagging reminder that maybe being human is better than being a demon. To convince themselves otherwise, they plan the grand finale in order to make a mockery of these characteristics.

• **They're bored of your emotions**

Psychopaths love the idealize phase because everything is perfect. There are no problems, and they don't have to deal with anyone's dreaded emotions. But after they've tricked someone into falling in love with them, they suddenly find themselves in a strange predicament. Their victim loves them and wants to foster a greater emotional connection. The psychopath gets bored & uncomfortable with this very quickly. In these cases, the grand finale will often be about the victim being crazy, bipolar, or hysterical. Again, these are all a flattering way of saying: "Hey, you have a heart." But psychopaths hate things they do not not understand, so they seek to destroy you. While you were spending so much time trying to repress your emotions to be the perfect partner, you were actually doing just fine all along as a regular person. Emotions are what make you human, and the psychopath got very tired of those human qualities.

Everything the psychopath values is the opposite of what you would value. So when they punish you, they're actually giving quite a tribute to the things you probably care about most. It's twisted & manipulative, because they convince you to doubt your greatest qualities—but looking back, you can begin to understand how this abuse was a subtle acknowledgment of your own strengths.

Granted, you probably don't want to hear any of that right now. After the grand finale, there is no hope. No humor. No future. You have been deeply wounded by the pain this person inflicted upon you, and it will take years to fully comprehend the extent of their abuse. So turn the page, and we will walk this road together.

THE STAGES OF GRIEF

Healing from psychopathic abuse is a long journey.
It is neither linear nor logical. You can expect to swing
back and forth between stages, perhaps even inventing a few
of your own along the way. It is unlike the traditional stages
of grief, because you have not truly lost anything—instead,
you have gained everything. You just don't know it yet.

Devastation

Symptoms: Emptiness, shock, substance abuse,
suicidal thoughts, inability to focus, depression,
physical deterioration.

This is the stage immediately following the breakup, in
which you feel all-consuming devastation. Your heart and
mind become numb, unable to perform trivial tasks. You've
been ripped away from the chemical addiction going on in
your brain, so a lingering haze should be expected as you go
through the withdrawal process. Your body will physically
deteriorate—appearing fragile and haunted when you look at
yourself in the mirror. Before & after pictures of psychopathic abuse survivors are shocking.

Your sex drive will oscillate between desire for them and
the misery of thinking about what you no longer have. Psy-

chologically, you are extremely raw and vulnerable from the identity erosion, but at this point you aren't even aware that your identity was eroded. You don't yet understand the extent of their emotional abuse. So instead of healing from their tactics, you are still a victim of it all. You genuinely believe you deserve this—that you are nothing without them. That you are jealous, crazy, needy, clingy, and everything is your fault.

You feel worthless.

Spiritually, you will lose any connection you once had with the world around you. Your empathetic and perceptual abilities will temporarily collapse. Looking back, you will be unable to remember most of the details during this phase. Almost like an out-of-body experience, your mind will have blocked out many of the unbearably painful & embarrassing memories. A part of you shuts down in order to protect your spirit—the stages of grief are about bringing it to life again.

Taking Care of Yourself

During the entire healing process—but especially right now—you must remember to treat your body well. It's the least you can do, considering your mind is going to be out of commission for quite some time. Along the way, I'll outline some more suggestions. But here are some basic ideas to get you started:

- Practice meditation whenever you can. My beautiful friend & ice-skating partner, An Old-Fashioned Girl, has shared so many techniques on our website that you can try throughout the day. She offered one example where you simply take 10 deep breaths in a row—and you can do this anytime, anywhere!

- Take a multivitamin with B complex each day. This will ensure you're receiving all of the nutrients you need. B6 and B12 can also help to combat depression.

- Fish oil is an excellent supplement to keep your skin and hair strong, but it also has some great antidepressant qualities to it. Go buy yourself a bottle, it's really cheap.

- Go for a walk each day. The gym is most likely out of the question at this point, but you need to incorporate some sort of physical activity into your daily routine.

- Eat three meals each day, even when you're not hungry. You probably won't feel like eating for a few weeks. But you cannot starve your body, so keep yourself fed & healthy.

- Wake up at a reasonable hour each morning. You don't want to get stuck in the habit of rolling out of bed in the afternoon, too depressed to face the day. Set an alarm if you need to.

- Get 7-9 hours of sleep. Adequate rest is essential to your mental health, and you won't be able to get through this if you're exhausted every day.

- Go outside and get some sun. Wear sunscreen, of course—but enjoy the natural light of the outdoors, and absorb some vitamin D from the sun. You'll feel better.

- Take care of your basic hygiene each day. Don't skip out on brushing your teeth or taking a shower. The more you get into a routine, the easier it will become to form good habits.

- Get away from the mirror. Seriously, you look fine. The psychopath conditioned you to feel especially self-conscious about the way you look, but no one is judging you like they did.

Reflection

During the devastation period, you will find it very difficult to reflect on anything at all. But I must ask you to look inward, just for a moment—because this is the most important paragraph in the whole book. Many survivors struggle with suicidal thoughts, unable to imagine life beyond this experience. To cope with this, some begin to drink alone or abuse prescription pills. If you're self-medicating or considering suicide, please put this book down and seek professional counseling immediately. No healing resource can provide you with the help you need right now.

Once you understand that life is worth living, continue on.

Denial

Symptoms: Volatility, pseudo-happiness,
manic moods, substance abuse, impulsivity,
attention-seeking, cyberstalking.

You can expect this stage to start up in full force when the psychopath begins waving their happy life in your face. You see them running off with another partner, gleefully telling the world how flawless their life is now. This triangulation is commonly done through social media. At this point, you aren't even angry about the new target, because you likely have no idea how long the infidelity was going on. You just feel the need to prove that you are fine and dandy like the psychopath—because then maybe they'll want you back.

Keep that in the back of your mind: your healing is still largely centered around the psychopath desiring you again.

In order to convince yourself that everything is okay, you change jobs, spend money, and redefine your entire life. You lash out at everyone and everything except the psychopath. You go out drinking, partying, and dating recklessly—all in a monumental effort to convey the message that you are fine. You will become very impulsive, blowing away your savings and harboring delusional thoughts of returning to your idealizer. You may try to replicate the exact dynamic you had with the psychopath with another partner, only to get very frustrated that your sex life isn't as good or that they don't love-bomb you with attention.

You spend a lot of time online, accidentally peeking at their Facebook profile and learning about their new life. A part of you isn't ready or willing to believe that the relationship is actually over. You think if they just see one picture or comment of yours, then maybe they'll realize what a mistake they've made. But much to your dismay, they don't seem to be paying any attention to you at all. You might even invent situations in your mind where they secretly want you back. So you continue to act out, unaware that your sense of self has become entirely consumed by someone else. This is the phase in which you'll be most likely to do things you'll regret after recovery has ended.

Drinking

Please stop drinking. In the early months of recovery, this is the seemingly easiest way to deal with your pain. Downing a bottle of wine each night somehow becomes "normal"—and you defend it with excuses or a casual joke. But it's not funny. You are doing a lot of damage to your mind & body. If you're serious about healing, you need to be completely in touch with your sober, unaltered state of mind. You will find no peace from alcohol-induced rants, drunk storytelling, and mindless partying. These distractions only serve to delay your healing process. You will still have all of the same work to do once you wake up the next morning—and it'll be made substantially more difficult with a hangover and embarrassing stories from the night before.

There's nothing wrong with having a drink every now and then, but this experience is an exception. Spend a few months completely dry. Make a calendar if you need to, checking off each day as you go. You will be absolutely amazed at how quickly your healing process accelerates. Your mind is the most valuable tool in the recovery process—so treasure it and treat yourself kindly.

Making Big Decisions

One of the most humbling aspects about working in abuse recovery is that I can't tell anyone how to heal. Remember when you were a kid, your parents would give you a bunch of life lessons about how not to repeat their mistakes? So of course you ignored them, because no one can tell you how to be happy—no, you had to go off and make those very same mistakes yourself.

The stages of grief are exactly the same, but I still want to share some advice—on the off chance that it happens to resonate with you.

During the denial phase, you should avoid making big, life-changing decisions. You will invest your happiness into so many different things, unable to realize that happiness must first come from within. You will enthusiastically rip apart your life, confident that every idea you come up with is the next best solution.

But there is no solution.

There is nothing wrong with your job. There is nothing wrong with your salary. There is nothing wrong with your home, your phone, your profile picture, or your single status. None of these things are the problem—no, you've been long trained to ignore the real problem.

So in this stage, I strongly urge you to avoid making big decisions—especially ones involving money & friends. You will have plenty of time to sort out the friendship situation after you've gone through recovery. For now, you should **not** trust your gut instincts. Rarely will you ever hear me say that, but right now everything is out of balance. Your intuition is skewed, completely unhinged by the psychopath's abuse.

If you are suspicious of toxic friends, simply distance yourself from them for the time being. It does not need to be personal or unpleasant. Just tell them you're going through a difficult time, and you'll reconnect with them when you've found some peace. Then, you will be free to dedicate some time to recovery forums where you know people will understand what you're going through. Your old friends will not get it—but this does not necessarily make them bad people. They will simply suggest that you "move on", giving you the best breakup advice they know. Ask yourself: if you hadn't gone through this experience, would you know how to empathize with a survivor?

If, in one year, you still want that new job, or to send a nasty letter to a long-time friend, then go ahead and do it. But for now, your future self might be very grateful for your present self's patience.

Education & Self-Doubt

Symptoms: Uncertainty, anxiety, curiosity,
disbelief, excessive storytelling, self-blame,
contradicting yourself.

This is where things start to change really fast. Somehow,
you come across the topic of psychopathy or narcissism or
sociopathy. Whether it be through a lucky internet search,
some pre-existing life knowledge, or a skilled therapist, you
now have the biggest piece of the puzzle. This is why the
label matters. From here, everything starts to fall into place.

You know deep down that something within you is horribly broken. Even though you impatiently want to feel good
again, you also want to figure out what in the world just happened. When you begin to read through the red flags of psychopathy, you will experience extreme self-doubt. You will
recognize most—if not all—of the warning signs, but you
will wonder if you're just labeling your ex a psychopath because you cant handle the truth of how you ruined the relationship. This is, of course, **their** truth.

So you oscillate back and forth between your idealizer and
your abuser. How could someone who thought you were
perfect also be the very same person who intentionally hurt
you? How could they go from obsession to contempt in the

blink of an eye? It isn't possible. There's no way you dated a psychopath. They loved you. Right?

Cognitive Dissonance

What I've just described is a psychological phenomenon known as cognitive dissonance. It's a state of mind where your intuition is telling you two competing things. It's totally natural after a psychopathic relationship, because you're used to repeatedly being **told** things—instead of seeing them with your own two eyes, or feeling them in your heart. You constantly heard the psychopath make sweeping declarations of love and dedication, but you never actually felt it. You fondly remember the dreams you shared with them, and the future you planned together—but obviously those things didn't happen.

So what do you listen to? Their actions or their words? During the relationship, you probably spent a lot of time with their words. Cherishing them, idolizing them, analyzing them, and ultimately distrusting them. But despite your intuition telling you something was wrong, a part of you still desperately wanted to believe in the manufactured soul mate.

And now, you're unraveling these illusions. You don't fully understand how their mind works, but you know something wasn't quite right. So there's going to be a battle going on in your own mind—a battle to quell the dream of love & passion, so that you have a chance to see things rationally.

You will switch from one extreme to the other. First, they're a total monster who cheated & lied throughout the relationship. Then, they're really not the worst person in the world—they were insensitive, and definitely didn't hurt you intentionally. If you just forgive them, then maybe everyone could be happy. But wait, some of those things they said to you were really cruel. They made you feel like garbage, patronizing you as if you were a child. Then again, everyone deserves a second chance—you've always been taught not to hold grudges, and it'd be a lot more pleasant to remain friends with them. Plus, how could you forget those beautiful memories where you held hands as they said "I love you"...

And that's the danger of cognitive dissonance. It brings you back to the addictive love memories. It causes you to long for a broken dream—a manufactured lie. As you begin to work through these feelings, you will slowly come towards an equilibrium. The thoughts will become less and less extreme. But in the mean time, you are still very susceptible to their ongoing abuse. As long as you're experiencing cognitive dissonance, make no mistake: they will be able to trick you again. All it takes is one sweet word to trigger you right back to the idealization phase. So how can you protect yourself?

No Contact

After a relationship with a psychopath, No Contact is the only way to stay safe from their manipulation & abuse. There are **no** exceptions to this rule. No matter how badly you were hurt, contact will only make it worse. If you have children or other lasting connections to the psychopath, engage in the minimal amount of contact possible.

No Contact is exactly what it sounds like. It means you don't contact the psychopath in any way, shape or form. So what constitutes contact? More than you might think:

-Phone calls
-Text messages

-Seeing them in person
-Emails
-Facebook friendship
-Facebook messages
-Cyber-stalking

Nothing good can come from contact with a psychopath, now matter how seemingly insignificant the contact might be. It will greatly hinder your healing process and you will always regret it later on. Every bit of communication with the psychopath only serves to hurt you. They're always interested in triangulating you, but this can easily be mistaken as genuine care & interest. Given the chance, they will suck you back in with charm, only to resume the nightmare you remembered from the identity erosion. They will restore the idealize phase, triggering you back to cognitive dissonance. They will lie pathologically, driving you out of your mind. They will engage in word salad, uprooting your entire healing process.

Psychopaths are expertly skilled at creating fake personas for themselves. They will appear to be very happy with their new life without you, causing greater emotional damage. As soon as they get their claws around you again, you will get dragged back into their psychotic world. You must break free of this addiction—and the only way is through No Contact.

When your thoughts start to race, be aware of this. Realize that these thoughts do not make you happy and only dig you into a deeper depression. Find distractions for yourself. A new hobby, meditation, writing, work, a pet—anything to get your mind off of the psychopath. The brain learns habits. So teach it healthier ones. When you notice your mind going back to the psychopath, take a deep breath and force yourself to think about other things.

The same goes for cyber-stalking. Even though you're not directly communicating with them, you're still indulging an addiction. The only way to break that addiction is to cut off every channel with them, cold turkey. You can do it now by blocking them on Facebook, Twitter, and your cell phone plan.

You may think you'll feel better if you stick around to see their next target get dumped like you. But you won't. Nothing will change the pain you feel, except time & personal growth. Believe it or not, you will reach a period when you could not care less about what they are doing or who they're courting.

If you've had enough of me, take it from one of our very first members, DawnG. She is totally awesome, and her wisdom can help all of us:

"This method of taking back your life and sanity is accepted and recommended by virtually all professionals helping people cope with abusive, manipulative relationships. Here's why this is the only way to go forward: you cannot begin healing your wounds until you break free from the fog of confusion their disorder creates around the people closest to them. You cannot break completely free from that confusion until you back off and give yourself a chance to think rationally again.

Here are the ground rules:

1.   No calls, no texts, no emails, no Facebook, no Twitter. Stop looking at their Facebook pages. Stop creeping on their friends' Facebook pages. Un-friend and block them from viewing your page. Block their phone numbers and their email addresses.

2.   No "accidental" meetings. Stay away from the places they go.

3.   Avoid places that remind you of him/her.

4.   Don't discuss them with mutual friends and acquaintances. You may have to ask people to stop telling you things. Don't keep tabs on their life—and don't give them the means to keep tabs on you. It's also a very bad idea to contact their exes and family members. Really, don't do this. The risk of this blowing up in your face is too high.

5.   Get rid of reminders. It probably isn't enough to just pack away photos and such. You know you'll go digging through boxes later. Delete emails, texts, and photos from your phone and computer. Get rid of the stuff that they left behind. Get rid of the gifts they gave you in "good times"—all two or three of them. **Delete this fake relationship from your life**. It wasn't real. It wasn't love. It wasn't mutual respect and caring. Do you really want to keep physical reminders of something so bad?

6.   Do not take the bait. Many psychopaths continue calling, texting, emailing, or leaving voicemails after you've expressed that you want no more contact. These messages may be sweet and nostalgic, or they may be cruel and obscene. They may express a wish to "negotiate" your return. They might make beautiful promises. Remember that these people cannot change—you're going to end up in another battle for control and you will be the loser. It's inevitable. If the psychopath contacts

you with accusations, please understand this is bait and they want you to defend yourself so that they can keep you engaged. Find the resolve to resist engaging, even when they ramp up the attention. This is an attack on your new boundaries and they may be determined for a while to break those boundaries. They don't miss you, they miss controlling you and messing with your mind. That deep sorrow, that overwhelming feeling of loss they're expressing—it seems so genuine, but that isn't real. They're panicking because they lost control and they want desperately to get it back. To get **you** back in line.

7. Avoid alcohol and any other mind-altering substances. One of the worst things you can do is go on an alcohol-fueled, middle of the night rant on their voicemail, or show up at their house drunk and demanding answers. Do you want to prove their smear campaign accusations that you're out of control and crazy? Do you want to get drunk and end up either in their bed, or some other predator's, because you've dulled your inhibitions? No, you don't. As an added reason to avoid alcohol, many of these substances only contribute to existing anxiety and depression. Put the bottle away.

8. Reconnect with yourself, your family, your friends and your life. If you are suffering from severe emotional disturbances, seek the help of a licensed mental health professional with training and experience in abusive relationships. You don't have to deal with all of this by yourself. Talk to people. That's why we're here.

9. Don't contact them that one last time to let them know you know they're a psychopath, an abuser, a pathological liar, and a complete wanker. Really, they don't care what they are.

We understand that people have children with psychopaths and are required to maintain "low contact" in co-parenting situations. We understand that some of you have unfinished financial business that has to be completed and are also required to go low contact. We understand that some of you work with psychopaths. There are ways to implement emotional low contact with them until you finally can go completely No Contact in the future. This is still the ultimate goal, even if it takes time to get there.

Are you financially dependent on a psychopath? Are they controlling all of the money, keeping you from working while you cater to their needs, so that you cannot leave? Have you been conditioned to believe you have no options?

Nothing could be further from the truth.

You **do** have options, even if they don't seem particularly enticing at the moment. It's far better to move temporarily to a women's shelter than to stay in a relationship where you are constantly abused, belittled, controlled, and manipulated by a person whose end goal is your complete capitulation and emotional destruction.

Every single one of us who has gone No Contact will tell you that it's not easy. It takes real commitment to yourself and your own well-being. It's incredibly difficult to maintain in the beginning, but it does get exponentially easier as time goes on. The longer you stay out, the easier it becomes to find yourself again, or perhaps to find a new, healthier you. Many of us will tell you quite honestly that we don't have any desire to speak with the psychopath now. It's over. Done."

Resources

As you educate yourself, information flow is essential. This is the time to get overloaded with knowledge, books, and videos. You'll find some that you like, and others that you don't. The important thing is, find a lot of them. Later on, you'll probably feel comfortable settling down with a few favorite resources, but now is the opportunity to try them all.

Our goal at PsychopathFree is to help you heal in the best way possible. That could be through this book & our site, or it could be through hundreds of other resources out there. This section is a rapid-fire way to get new survivors up to speed on how much information is available on the topic.

- **Search Terms**

There are a lot of terms besides "psychopath" that might yield some very helpful resources. Here are some of the most common words that could help you in your search:

-Psychopath
-Sociopath
-Narcissist
-Narcissistic Personality Disorder (NPD)
-Anti-Social Personality Disorder (ASPD)
-Borderline Personality Disorder (BPD)
-Emotional Abuse
-Psychological Abuse
-Psychological Maltreatment
-Emotional Rape
-Covert Abuse
-Emotional Manipulator

-Cluster-B Personality Disorders

-Psychopathology

-Emotional Vampire

- **Websites**

We do not necessarily endorse any of these sites or blogs, but we believe all survivors should have access to every resource out there. It is up to you decide what helps or does not help your healing process.

-PsychopathFree.com: Articles & Recovery Forums

-PsychopathyAwareness.wordpress.com: Blog & Articles

-MelanieToniaEvans.com: Articles

-SamVak.tripod.com: Articles

-LoveFraud.com: Blog, Articles, & Recovery Forums

-NarcissismFree.com: Articles

-SaferelationshipsMagazine.com: Articles

-AlexandraNouri.com: Articles

- DaughtersOfNarcissisticMothers.com: Articles

-TheAbilityToLove.wordpress.com: Articles

- **Facebook Groups**

Facebook groups & pages are an amazing way to connect with other survivors, but you have to be careful since you are posting with your personal profile. Additionally, you must beware of trolls on these pages. There are a lot of good people out there, but there can also be some drama.

-After Narcissistic Abuse - There is Light, Life, & Love

-Narcissistic Abuse Recovery Central

-Respite from Sociopathic Behavior
-PsychopathFree

• **Icons & Figures**

There are several major educators and researchers in the field. Keep in mind that your understanding of psychopathy does not have anything to do with formal education or training—all it takes is one life experience.

-Claudia Moscovici
-Melanie Tonia Evans
-Robert Hare
-Martha Stout
-Sam Vaknin
-Sandra Brown
-Donna Andersen
-Steve Becker

• **Books**

There are many books written on the topic of psychopathy. Check out some of our favorites, along with the most popular ones out there. Remember that not every resource will be right for you.

-Dangerous Liaisons (Claudia Moscovici)
-The Seducer (Claudia Moscovici)
-The Sociopath Next Door (Martha Stout)
-In Sheep's Clothing (George Simon)
-Women Who Love Psychopaths (Sandra Brown)
-How to Spot a Dangerous Man (Sandra Brown)

-Without Conscience (Robert Hare)

-Snakes in Suits (Paul Babiak)

-Narcissistic Lovers (Cynthia Zayn)

-The Wizard of Oz and Other Narcissists (Eleanor Payson)

-Help! I'm In Love With a Narcissist (Steven Carter)

-What Makes Narcissists Tick (Kathy Krajco)

-Malignant Self-Love (Sam Vaknin)

-Love Fraud (Donna Andersen)

- **Articles**

For an extended collection of links, articles, & videos, please check out our master list—and feel free to contribute any that we missed:

Resources.PsychopathFree.com

Hopefully, this section has provided you with some useful tools to jumpstart your journey. Spreading awareness is the best way to help others out of the dark. Knowledge is power to survivors, and poison to psychopaths. The more information you have, the better. And once it all begins to sink in—well, then you're really in for something.

Understanding the Psychopath

Symptoms: Physical sickness, validation,
shock, disgust, "ah-hah" moments, paranoia,
sinking feeling in your chest.

This is one of the strangest & most important stages in
the healing process. Education can only take you so far—you
need to actually feel what the psychopath feels. Most victims
live by values of compassion and love, so it's nearly impossible to imagine empathizing with a psychopath. In fact, this is
why they're able to get away with so much—because normal
human beings automatically project their consciences onto
everyone else. Psychopaths do the opposite.

As you delve deeper into articles and research, you will in-
advertently lose a bit of yourself. You will become so consumed by psychopathy that you'll actually begin to understand how their minds work. Not just the red flags and verbal
abuse, but the sadistic pleasure they felt when they destroyed
you. The silence—even laughter—that you received when
you were begging and crying. Instead of excusing everything
as insensitive or dense, you look back on the relationship and
view all of their behavior from a very different perspective.

And suddenly everything clicks.

It all makes sense, when it never did before. From the mirroring to the love-bombing to the identity erosion to the triangulation to the eventual abandonment. You feel disgusted. You realize you were never loved—just another target in a never-ending cycle. You start to see that you've never behaved like this in any other relationship, and it's not because they were special. It's because they were actively working against you from the moment they chose you.

You look back at all of the things that once made you feel paranoid, now able to see that every instance of abuse & neglect was calculated and intentional. And finally, you come to the horrifying realization that the love of your life—the person you trusted with all your heart—had set you up for failure since the very beginning.

Intention & Sadism

One of the greatest myths surrounding psychopaths is this Hollywood pseudo-psychology that psychopaths are actually victims themselves. Whether it be an abusive past, an absent father, or something in between—the idea is that psychopaths cannot help their behavior. Sort of like depression, addiction, bipolar disorder, or autism.

This is flat-out wrong.

Unlike any other mental disorder, psychopaths are keenly aware of the impact that their behavior has on others. That's half the fun for them—watching you suffer. They pick up on insecurities and vulnerabilities in a heartbeat, and then make the conscious choice to exploit those qualities. They know right from wrong, and simply choose to steamroll straight through it.

The psychopathic relationship cycle is not some accidental byproduct of insensitivity and emotional thickness. It is a calculated, personalized process that psychopaths use to methodically torture their victims. To watch the kind & cheerful fall from grace, for no other reason than some easy entertainment.

You must imagine the time and planning that goes into mirroring someone else's hopes and dreams. They spend months—sometimes years—playing the role of a completely different person. All for one end game: your destruction. They did not feel any glimpse of love with you, even when they claimed you were the only one who ever made them feel this way. No, the entire time, they were just watching and observing you. Patiently waiting for the fun to start. Did you notice as soon as you fell in love and became comfortable in the relationship, that's when the emotional abuse started? From there, you spent the rest of the relationship frantically trying to revitalize the soul mate they once pretended to be.

The problem is, many survivors equate their insatiable drive for attention with some sort of childlike insecurity. But they are not insecure. They love themselves. They love the way they look, the way they can trick everyone around them, and the way you begged for them. You were not fulfilling some sort of void within their broken soul. They have no soul. They wanted to be worshipped and nothing else. They're not a lost little boy or girl hiding behind a tough persona—and their disorder is not a defense mechanism for deep-seated fragilities. You're never going to find a "soft spot" within them. Just endless darkness.

At some point, you must stop thinking along the lines of "I'll go No Contact because it'll take away their narcissistic supply." This implies that you still (or ever did) fulfill some sort of personal need within them. You don't, and you never will. They do not seek out attention from others to inflate their ego. It's already fully inflated, and I can assure you it'll never deflate.

They want your attention so that they can consume you, and then destroy you. Forget about supply. They saw you as disposable trash. And given the chance, they might recycle you, but it's **never** because they need you.

And what's more, your healing process should not revolve around giving or withholding attention from someone else. You should be going No Contact because you genuinely believe that you deserve better. This is someone who manipulated, lied, abused, and deeply hurt you. As you develop self-respect, you should come to understand that this is all more than enough reason to remove someone from your life—permanently.

Am I a Psychopath?

Too often, survivors come to the very disconcerting conclusion that they might be a psychopath. After months of studying the topic and thinking about the experience, I think it's only natural that you begin to question yourself and your own good nature. It's a nasty topic, even addictive at times. Like any part of the body, the brain learns habits—when your mind constantly bounces back to psychopathy, it's normal that you apply your knowledge to nearly everyone in your life, including yourself.

I've come up with several reasons that you are probably not a psychopath, because the last thing you need during the healing process is some nagging doubt that you're evil. You don't need this worry—and that's the key word here: worry. A psychopath would never worry about this. And moreover, they just don't care. You're scared because you see psychopathy as the root of all evil. But they don't see their disorder as the terrible sickness that it is. They see it as a strength. They believe their lack of conscience makes them superior. Do you think like that? I'm going to guess not. So here are the main reasons you're probably asking the question:

- **The psychopath made you feel this way**

Throughout the relationship, the psychopath projects their flaws onto you. They call you needy, jealous, clingy, controlling, evil, and crazy. This is all projection. Have you ever felt that way in any normal relationship or friendship? Do you feel that way around your Constant? No. So what is the common denominator here? Those are all characteristics of psychopathy, and it's no coincidence that they slowly disappear as you spend more time away from them.

Victims tend to absorb all of the problems in a relationship, believing that they can forgive and understand everything in order to save the perfect idealize phase. But in doing so, you end up absorbing many of their most horrible flaws, causing you to believe that you actually have those traits. After the identity erosion and grand finale, it is only natural to feel disgusted with yourself and your behavior—because you haven't been yourself. You became a receptacle for the psychopath's poison. But with time and No Contact, you begin to see that you don't display any of those characteristics when you're not around them. In fact, you seem to become more gentle, empathetic, and compassionate—closer to your most genuine self. That is the real you. The pseudo-psychopathic you was nothing more than a dumping ground for their most terrible traits. That's why you don't ever repeat these patterns in future relationships—while they most certainly do, every single time. Again, you must ask yourself who is the common denominator?

- **Your personality type**

There's this old saying that goes: "Don't believe everything you think." This is extremely important to remember in the aftermath of the grand finale. Most survivors tend to share a variety of common personality traits, two of them being open-mindedness & susceptibility to suggestions. These two qualities are actually great strengths, but they can also cause problems if you don't introspect a bit and learn to control them. The issue is, when you ask "am I a psychopath", your open mind will automatically entertain the idea. That's not because there's any rational reason to believe you're a psychopath, it's just because you have an open mind. That's it. When your mind suggests something to you, you listen. And sometimes, you just need to teach yourself to laugh it off as the ridiculous notion that it is.

Unfortunately, many survivors also tend to be very open to suggestions that they themselves are awful—and closed off to suggestions that someone else might be awful. As you recover and begin to reach your equilibrium again, you stop seeing things through such a selfless eye. That's not to say you become selfish, it just means you adopt more of an "I'm okay, you're okay" mentality. Instead of the toxic "I'm not okay, you're okay" that dominated most of your relationship. So just remember that you have an open mind and are likely to be much more susceptible to hypnosis and suggestions than other personality types. Be aware of this, and learn how to channel it.

Along these lines, depression is a crippling disease, but it's also strangely logical. During depression, negative thoughts find a way to stay in your mind by convincing your brain that they are more important than the positive thoughts. Just like a virus, depression develops survival mechanisms. It convinces you that your positive thoughts are just delusions and ignorance. This is especially difficult for any survivor high in the guilt area, because depression can take an entirely ridiculous idea and make you think it's real. But it's not. You are not a psychopath. Those negative thoughts running crazy in your mind are not real. Your brain is playing tricks on you.

- **You have boundaries**

You are probably not accustomed to having boundaries. In fact, many survivors never had boundaries to begin with. A strange gift from the psychopathic experience is that you begin to find these boundaries. Some call it healthy narcissism, but I think self-respect is a better term. The problem is, boundaries & self-respect are completely foreign to you at this point. So when you begin to express these things, you feel like a selfish, abrasive jerk. When in reality, you've just stopped playing the role of a selfless doormat.

You may begin to find that old friendships & toxic dynamics fall apart as you become stronger. It almost feels as if you're being punished for healing. But that's not the case. You're not psychopathic or narcissistic for having boundaries and expecting a decent level of respect in return. You're just a regular human being with feelings. But you may be surrounded by people who don't want you to be regular— they prefer the person who caters to their every need. So they make you feel bad for taking on healthier habits. This kind of conditioning can make you feel psychopathic and unempathetic, but again, that is not the case. That's what happens when selfish people stop getting their way. They fight for the status quo, because the existing dynamic suits them. But it doesn't suit you, and that's what boundaries help you realize. Just because you have to tell someone off or demand a bit of respect does not make you psychopathic. It makes you stronger. Every time you stand up for yourself, a part of your spirit comes back to life.

- **You experienced the relationship cycle for yourself**

The manufactured soul mate is not human. It is demented, twisted, and evil. Idealize, devalue, discard—every single time. But they're not the only one who feels those things throughout the relationship. You experience them too. The difference is in the order. You idealize them, more than you have idealized anyone in your life. Then, you are discarded, left broken and alone to pick up pieces. And finally, you begin to devalue them as you learn about psychopathy. You deconstruct the person from the grooming phase, just like they deconstructed you during the identity erosion.

This is not a natural cycle for any person to go through after a breakup. Sure, plenty of exes end up disliking each other. But no normal exes go through such a rollercoaster of highs and lows, deconstructing personality traits they once idealized. In normal relationships, flaws are flaws and strengths are strengths. In a psychopathic relationship, their strengths are fake and your flaws are manufactured.

Unfortunately, the only way to heal is to go through this toxic cycle yourself. Only then will you finally manage to see that it was all false. An illusion. A perverted mirror. In order to do so, you must begin the unnatural process of undoing everything you once loved. Not just some of it. All of it. Because none of it was ever real. Only then can you find self-respect and reclaim your dreams.

Additionally, you will go through many other devaluing processes that you don't experience in normal relationships. Many survivors cyberstalk for a while, mainly because they have absolutely no idea what just happened. Social networking provides an opportunity to gain some more insight into the truth and their next target, but eventually you must realize that it is not helpful in your healing process. The bottom line is, cyberstalking counts as Contact, and it doesn't do you any good. You probably got addicted to cyberstalking during the idealize phase, when you isolated yourself and waited desperately by the computer for their every update. They knew this and loved the power it gave them. But they were doing the same thing as you, although they were probably much better at hiding it. For instance, they might have claimed that they barely ever checked your Facebook feed anymore, and then accidentally referenced something you posted a few days ago. Or they might have said they weren't expecting your call, when they were actually wondering what took you so long. So don't beat yourself up for getting caught up in the mind games. Just understand that this addiction is unhealthy, and that self-control can finally put an end to it.

During and after the psychopathic relationship, you've probably done things you're not proud of—you've lied, sought attention, and sent off angry emails. That doesn't make you a psychopath. At some point, you need to forgive yourself and make the conscious effort to start making better choices. You are not that nasty, stalking, mirroring, vengeful ex. It takes a lot of time and effort to purge your system of the toxic relationship cycle, but you can get there, and you can seek out normal, loving relationships.

- **Your empathy is completely destabilized**

You will feel empty and numb for long periods of time. That is the nature of psychopathic recovery. But numbness does not equal psychopathy. It means your emotions were raped and it's going to take a long time for them to come back again. Yes, a psychopath is emotionally numb, but they are that way for life. They would never spend months mourning the loss of their own innocence or ruminating about their broken heart.

Your emotions & empathy are just in hibernation. And one day, the sleeping bear will wake up stronger than ever. When all is said and done, you will find yourself more perceptive and compassionate than ever before. So don't worry about feeling numb right now. It goes away, and it's replaced by something much better.

Remember my recommendation that you wait several months before forming new friendships & relationships? The reason is that you'll feel frustrated and depressed because you can't seem to reach the same love or high that you had with the psychopath. You'll feel like a bad person for getting annoyed that your partner doesn't seem to be as attentive and sensual. You can't keep getting caught up in these post-psychopathic relationships, because they only harm you and the people around you. You will be overwhelmed with guilt, on top of your already damaged empathy.

So instead of beating yourself up for being unable to accomplish the impossible, spend some time introspecting and becoming your own best friend. Even introspection has its limits—at some point you must stop thinking and start living. This might take years, but you will know in your heart when you're ready. Too much introspection can drive a person mad. But just the right amount can bring about all sorts of wisdom and creativity

- **You have a heightened understanding of human nature**

A lot of survivors once walked through this world believing that all people had some amount of good in them. The psychopath served as a nasty wakeup call from that blissful ignorance. As you learn more about psychopathy, you also learn more about human nature. You understand how and why the psychopath tricked you—how they played on your greatest insecurities. How they love-bombed you. How they set off a chemical addiction.

And then suddenly, you might feel a little bit dark inside. It's like you've come too close to evil. And now you know how human beings think—how you could flatter someone into doing anything for you. Or how you could make someone feel suicidal. It's some really nasty knowledge that you'd probably prefer not to have. But think about it, would you ever act on it? Of course not. Your conscience would stop you in a heartbeat. That's what separates you from the psychopaths. Not the knowledge, but your conscience & resulting actions. So no, you are not evil for having this new understanding of people and the world.

J.K. Rowling wrote: "We've all got both light and dark inside us. What matters is the part we choose to act on. That's who we really are." Keep that in mind during your healing process. Every person has their own demons—what defines us is how we choose to handle them.

Recall the blissful days when you knew nothing about psychopathy. Life was good. Did you ever feel evil for enjoying a compliment? Manipulative for being kind? Ill-intentioned for doing a good deed? My guess is no. It's only when you encountered something so sinister that you began to question yourself. Well, enough already. You are not a psychopath, and you never were. Like everything else, the brain heals and you will find your equilibrium again as your empathy & emotions come back to life.

You've been conditioned to see compliments and attention as some sort of weapon, but they're not. Appreciating a compliment or enjoying some attention every now and then does not make you a psychopath. You need to feel comfortable accepting these things from normal, healthy people. Don't let your understanding of how you were manipulated stop you from enjoying one of the nicest things in life: positive energy.

You are not a psychopath. You're the polar opposite. And that's the only reason you're asking this question in the first place.

Delayed Emotions

Symptoms: Rage, depression, extreme jealousy,
racing thoughts, hatred, overwhelming
temptation to contact them.

Once you understand the psychopath, you're going to experience a lot of unpleasant emotions. So get comfortable,
because you're going to be here for a while.

In this stage, you will begin to feel all of the things you
weren't allowed to feel during the relationship. Remember
the emotions you brushed aside in order to maintain peace
with them? Those didn't actually go anywhere—they just
stirred around in your heart for a while, manifesting as self-
doubt and anxiety. But now that you finally understand how
their games work, you're absolutely sickened. You feel
tricked. Manipulated. Violated.

Rage

Your self-doubt is replaced by anger. You know the truth.
You see how you were used, groomed, and brainwashed.
You're beyond angry. You want to murder them. You want
to contact everyone in their life and tell them what they did.

You want to write them a letter and tell them to burn in hell. You obsessively talk about it with your friends and family— you need to get your story out there. You've been shut up and minimized for so long, and now your voice is finally free.

Whenever you accused them of cheating or lying, they would turn it around and blame it on you, so you felt bad instead of mad. This cognitive dissonance caused a huge displacement of anger. You feel delayed emotions of jealousy as you realize how long the cheating was going on—how they used your manufactured behavior to court someone else with sympathy & pity. The smear campaign makes you feel the need to prove and defend yourself.

This delayed rage is completely expected after a psychopathic relationship. It can take months, even years to feel. Please, if possible, do not act on it. You will only prove their point. The greatest thing you can do is remain calm and composed. They want you to feel rage so they can show everyone how crazy you are—and how much you still love them. They will use you for triangulation long after the relationship has ended, even when you go No Contact.

And what's more, anger can only take you so far. It's an essential part of the healing process, but it won't bring you any long-term peace. Its main purpose is to develop your self-respect—an understanding that you deserved so much better.

Depression

You will swing back and forth between depression and rage for a very long time, in no particular order. You'll have good days and bad days, unable to maintain any sort of consistency in your moods. One night, you will think you're ready to move on—the next morning, you'll wake up crying and screaming into a pillow.

You don't want to be sad. And you don't deserve to be mad. All you did was fall in love. Why are you being punished for falling in love?

You find it impossible to go anywhere without thinking about your abuser. Every couple you come across reminds you of your lost relationship. Your old love songs seem to come up on the radio every second of the day. You can't even have a glass of wine without bursting into tears and embarrassing yourself.

And so you begin to isolate from the world around you, surrounding yourself with people who understand you on discussion forums. You have obsessive, racing thoughts. The tiniest things set you off. Your boundaries are returning—or perhaps being formed for the very first time—and you can't believe you let yourself sink so low. Only now are you beginning to realize how much you truly lost. How much you uprooted in your own life to make room for them. Not just friends, money, and life experiences—but also your happiness. Your kind understanding of the world has been shattered. Instead of giving people the benefit of the doubt, you suddenly have trouble trusting.

You begin to notice a constant feeling of dread and tightness in your chest. The demon that wraps its claws around your heart, always there to remind you of everything you want to forget.

Stop the Obsessing

The temptation to contact them becomes almost overwhelming in this stage. Plenty of survivors go the route of exposure, usually because they are consumed by the delayed emotions. Some post on cheater sites, others warn the next target. Some might even start a website. If you did any of that, don't beat yourself up. There's no right way to go about all of this. At the other end of the table, survivors who never contact the psychopath again are often left wishing they had taken some sort of revenge.

You see? Either way—justice or no justice—you're not going to be happy with the aftermath. There is no closure with psychopathic relationships, only acceptance.

In the meantime, there are ways to quell your racing thoughts. You don't want your brain to get into the permanent habit of thinking like this. DawnG provides some great advice on overcoming the dread & obsession often felt during this time:

"I'm not a professional but I want to try to explain intrusive thoughts as they were explained to me. The brain is a very complex organ. You have memories stored and feelings attached to those memories. Very strong feelings also have an affect on the rest of your body—they're all connected. So when you see this person, or think about them in your daily life, your brain pulls up strong feelings and memories that have an effect on the whole of you. They replay in your mind until your brain literally rewires itself and keeps those 'tracks' replaying, over and over again. And before you know it, you're stuck with intrusive thoughts that you don't want.

The way to stop them is to retrain your brain to think of other things—to rewire the neurons into playing healthier tracks. What you want is the reality of **right now**. Do this however you can. It helps immensely to keep busy with things that take conscious thought, and by forcing your brain to see the reality of the situation with your abuser.

My therapist told me to start telling my brain 'No' and 'Stop' very forcefully. This person who did cruel things to you is not a good person—you want to get away from them. So why would you want to keep caring about what they're thinking or doing?

It's not easy, but it certainly can be done. I would say that all of us who have been here long-term have done it rather successfully, even if it was a subconscious effort."

Complex PTSD

Symptoms: Numbness, feeling of disconnect, flashbacks, triggering memories, aversion to love & sex, two 'you's, isolation.

Once you've felt all the emotions you needed to feel, your spirit will be left broken. Exhausted. Because when all is said and done, you know you can't remain angry and depressed forever. There comes a point when it's no longer healthy venting—just addictive rumination. You know you'll never get back together with them, and you understand that you cannot change the past.

So what comes next? How do you go back to your daily life, learning to cope with the abuse you suffered? How do you enjoy each day without the excessive flattery and approval that you'd grown so accustomed to? Something about the world just seems different now. Lifeless. Dull. Hopeless.

You find that you're set off by the most obscure triggers, unable to enjoy a date or some time with an old friend. You're on high alert the entire time, constantly looking out for manipulation & red flags. The slightest jokes will offend you. That feeling of dread in your heart never seems to go away—warning you that anyone and everyone could be out to hurt you.

And then, after you spend time with others, you over-analyze the experience and come up with a list of reasons that this person shouldn't be in your life anymore. Then you feel awful for thinking those things, guilty and ashamed that you could be so disloyal. Your opinions of others will oscillate back and forth, just like they did for the psychopath. You are now applying the horror you experienced to every aspect of your life, even though they have been gone for quite some time now.

Contrary to popular belief, you do not need to be a war veteran or a kidnapping victim to suffer from PTSD. Your current situation fits every one of the criteria for this disorder:

- **Exposure to a traumatic event**. Yes, relationship abuse from someone you love is traumatic and life-altering.
- **Persistent re-experiencing**. Yes, through the mean and sweet cycle, you were repeatedly subjected to their abuse.
- **Persistent avoidance and emotional numbing**. Yes, this is the coping mechanism you adopted to excuse their behavior.
- **Persistent symptoms of increased arousal not present before**. Yes, you begin to feel these during the delayed emotions stage, ultimately manifesting as anxiety and fear.
- **Duration of symptoms for more than 1 month**. Yes, most survivors will require anywhere from 12-24 months of recovery before they begin to trust & love again.

- **Significant impairment**. You tell me—how do you feel right about now? I'd say impaired is an understatement.

As you come to understand that your brain chemicals were altered by this experience, you should feel comfortable seeking out professional help from those who know how to combat this debilitating obstacle in the healing process. There is no shame in mental illness—all you need to worry about is finding the right help for **you**. I personally had the best experience working with a therapist who specialized in relationship abuse. My time with her was life-changing, and she's responsible for so much of the peace I feel now. Keep in mind, there are also bad "professionals" out there. If you do choose to speak with someone, remember you have every right to like or dislike them. There are going to be dozens of opportunities in your area, so do not settle for someone unless you feel 100% satisfied. Trust your intuition when it comes to finding the perfect match.

New Pain After the Darkness

After the psychopathic experience, life seems to stand still for a while. You pour all of your energy into research, validation, and healing. The world around you stops while you work to regain a sense of self. But inevitably, life goes on. And as such, painful things continue to happen. Whether it be death, another breakup, loss of a beloved pet, an illness, or anything in between, you will experience pain. But after the psychopath, it's different. You find yourself always going back to this: "I could have coped with this so much better if that psychopath thing had never happened."

You burden yourself with more misery, finding that each challenge seems to lead you back to that one, even if it's totally unrelated.

This is especially true for breakups, where you had a glimmer of hope & joy with someone else—an experience that finally made you forget about the psychopath. And once that's gone, the feelings come rushing back, like a second wave of the identity erosion, even though they are long gone.

I don't believe these feelings actually have anything to do with the psychopath. Your spirit has transformed, becoming more sensitive and vulnerable to sadness. You might initially interpret this as a bad thing, because it makes you feel weak when you need strength the most.

But this negative energy you're feeling has a bigger & more important purpose. Instead of digging through old memories, allow yourself to let go. Cry as much as you want to. Send out waves of loving energy, to heal where it is needed, or to touch what is already gone. You will find yourself exhausted, but also at peace, connected to something deeper than yourself.

Dealing with grief will never be the same again, but that doesn't have to be a bad thing. It only feels bad at first because you have no idea where to direct all of these new & overwhelming emotions. So you go back to what feels familiar—when you felt the absolute worst.

Here's another thing to keep in mind when you're feeling down: how many other things have become easier to cope with because of this whole experience? Most survivors find better friendships, healthier relationships, self-respect, boundaries, and a broader connection with humanity.

Negativity can work like a rolling snowball sometimes, and it's important to remember how far you've come. Give yourself some credit for pulling yourself out from the ashes.

You thrived from darkness. You do not need to fear it anymore.

Embarrassment

After making it through the early, ugly stages of grief, many victims feel ashamed of themselves and the relationship aftermath. They cannot believe they sunk so low, actually begging another human being for acceptance & approval. It feels like an insult to your soul, and rightfully so.

To make matters worse, you probably spent a lot of time defending yourself to anyone who would listen—waging imaginary arguments and trying to explain your changed position about the relationship. Telling others that they weren't actually the perfect partner you once claimed them to be, but instead an abusive psychopath.

Unknowingly, survivors often continue to seek approval from external sources long after the relationship has ended. It's a habit that you picked up after placing all of your self-worth into the psychopath's oscillating opinions. When you continue these patterns with others, you might end up with some embarrassing memories—especially if you had always prided yourself on being independent and positive.

It's sort of like a big dark cloud over your otherwise good track record. Your life became a bag of marbles, spilling all over the floor. Your thoughts & emotions scattered everywhere, making it impossible to find clarity and truth. Then slowly, over the course of many months, you began putting the marbles back into the bag. The longer you did this, the more you started to understand what really happened and how your behavior might have come across to others.

But don't worry about this anymore. Forgive yourself and move on—everyone else has. Nobody thinks about you as much as you do. That might sound rude, but I think it's more humbling than anything else. It's a reminder that everyone fights their own battles every single day, and most people won't even remember the embarrassing thing you said a week ago unless you continually bring it up.

Your goal is to focus on the present. There are so many good things coming your way. You will discover more about yourself and this world than you could ever imagine. Because the thing about missing marbles is that you have to search in strange places to find them.

Cognitive Dissonance Returns

The old saying goes that time heals all wounds, and that's true to an extent. The problem with recovery progress is that it also encourages you to forget about how bad things really were during the relationship. It's a healing mechanism for your heart—selective amnesia to protect you from the painful memories. You might find yourself thinking about forgiveness and meeting up with them for lunch, just to find some peace from the whole thing.

Don't be mistaken, you will just be dragged right back into the same old mind games. You are only projecting your recovered state of happiness and optimism onto your memory of the relationship. This is actually healthy, because it helps to quell the racing thoughts. But you absolutely should not act on these improving moods. Take note of the progress as a tribute to your own efforts. Understand that you are feeling better **because** of your time spent away from the psychopath—not because you're ready to seek closure. Bringing them back into your life will only throw you right back to the earlier stages.

I will go into much greater detail about forgiving your abuser in the final chapter of this book. For now, your only job is to continue No Contact and treat yourself kindly.

Trauma & the Two Worlds

One of the most bizarre parts of recovery is feeling as if there are "two you's". The cheerful, trusting soul from before the abuse. And the abrasive, paranoid mess that you fear you've now become. But I think there's something else entirely going on here.

Instead of two you's, let's say there are two worlds. The material world that you see and hear every day. And then another one that you can feel only in your heart—a special connection with the universe & all beings. As kids, I think we're born with a natural link to both. But as we socialize and grow up, we develop a stronger preference for the first. Slowly, our connection with the quiet world weakens.

To make up for this, we begin to develop a powerful guard—something to keep us safe and confident in the world we've chosen. This guard takes care of our deepest insecurities, vanities, and failures. We learn to judge outwardly, instead of perceiving inwardly. Things are comfortable. From day one, we are developing this guard, teaching us how to be "strong". Strong, of course, being completely defined by the material world.

And then, throughout the course of life, adversity wears away at our guard like sandpaper—hardship, loss, and heartbreak. Slowly, we rebuild this connection with the other world, gaining wisdom and a gentle compassion for the people around us. We look back at our younger selves in embarrassment, wondering how we could have been so obnoxious. At least, that's how I imagine it goes.

But trauma is different.

Instead of sandpaper, the guard is shattered in a single moment. Whatever the damage, your guard is not nearly enough to save you from something so painful. So it collapses, and it can never be rebuilt.

During this brutal disconnect, you lash out and bring harm to others. You over focus on their behavior, unable to recognize your own—after all, this is what you've become accustomed to. You're dependent and needy, desperately latching on to anyone who will hear your story. You become numb to the things that once made you happy, fondly recalling an "old self" who seemed so much more cheerful.

You are indeed a mess. But in which world?

As you heal from your wounds, you begin to find peace in places you haven't explored since childhood. Imagination. Spirituality. Love. And I mean real love—not the narcissistic, hyper-validating garbage that we crave here. You start to fill your void with empathy & compassion, qualities that have been with you since the very beginning.

Mindless socialization doesn't do it for you anymore. You seek out deep, philosophical conversations with like-minded individuals. You often find that you don't fit into various social settings that you used to enjoy. You become frustrated when people don't understand why topics like psychopathy and empathy are so important. You forget that most people still live comfortably with their worldly guard—as you once did—and therefore remain unaffected by these issues.

You struggle between these two worlds, blaming it on the "two you's". You find that no matter how hard you try, you can never go back to that old self. The person who seemed so much happier and more innocent. But you also start to notice that your interactions with others are becoming much healthier. You've developed boundaries, self-respect, and self-worth. You do not need your worldly guard to be yourself, and that is a strange realization indeed.

And with time, you find that you don't need a guard to be happy at all. For once, self-respect actually comes from—well—the self. You see how much this universe has to offer to those who listen. And you exhaust less patience on the bothersome things in between.

As you become more comfortable with yourself, you see that your trauma did not destroy you. It ripped apart your guard and opened a connection with some other world—with all of humanity. You have not lost your childlike wonder. It has been with you all along, and now you are wise enough to live peacefully among both worlds. With joy and wisdom.

You can feel the pain of others, and therefore offer much deeper and more meaningful relationships. You understand that what you have is special, and cannot be simply shared with anyone. You find peace from listening to the quiet corners of the world. You do not mind time alone, for that is simply time in another world.

The most important thing to remember for all trauma survivors: there is nothing wrong with you. You are beautiful. You were thrown into an impossible situation, and you survived. Your innocence was taken away without your permission. You were violated. But in this violation, you regained something that takes most people a lifetime to find.

Your path may be painful, but it is also special. The universe has different plans for you. Remember, there are others who have permanently destroyed any path to the spiritual world. Psychopaths have no place there, and it is why they hate empathetic beings. You are a nagging reminder of something they will never find. They will die here in the material world, with no deeper connection to this great universe.

Sometimes, I believe the spirit world leaks into this one. You can feel it. An overwhelming sadness, when it is not your sadness. Joy for a friend, when it is not your joy. A strange "coincidence" when two people are thinking of one another. Even through this book, I believe we are all connected.

So now imagine these two worlds merging. A place where feelings & compassion are visible to the human eye. Where our spirits soar together like birds, singing songs with bright colors & glowing lights. We can see one another's pain—thorny vines wrapped around a troubled soul. The flickering lights in a victim's spirit.

This would be an incredible world for us, but not for the psychopaths. Because if the worlds merged, they would cease to exist.

So let us work together to bring these two worlds closer. To dismiss darkness, and to teach all empathetic human beings that they are beautiful. Never be ashamed of your abuse or your past. You are here now for a reason—and this is only the beginning.

The Loss of Innocence

Symptoms: Profound sadness, mourning, loneliness, acceptance, seeing the world in a different way, hope, accidental wisdom.

There is a difference between sadness and depression. Depression is hopeless, frightening, and mind-numbing. But sadness is beautiful—the gentle moment when your spirit prepares itself for a fresh start.

When you begin to feel real sadness, it's a sign that you're reaching the light at the end of the tunnel. Instead of devastating emptiness and upsetting triggers, your heart is ready to make one last transition. You're done mourning the loss of your soul mate—and instead, you are finally ready to mourn for yourself. You go from a perpetual state of thinking about someone else, to suddenly thinking about what **you** lost from all of this.

And most survivors find that they've lost a lot: friendships, money, career opportunities, self-esteem, health, and dignity. Fortunately, these things can all be repaired. You find that as you return to your roots, all of these things fall back into place. Some will even improve, especially future friendships and relationships.

But there's one thing you will never be able to get back: your innocence. Keep in mind that innocence has nothing to do with ignorance or naivety. It's simply the well-intentioned belief that all human beings have some good in them—the trust and love that you wholeheartedly gave to someone else. That's innocence.

Moving forward, you will never see the world like that again.

That's not to say you're now hypervigilant and jaded. It just means that you're going to view the world and the people around you in a more realistic light. Instead of automatically projecting your own goodness onto others, you let their actions speak for themselves. You see, this is not at all a bad thing. It's just sad at first, because you can never know you're losing your innocence until it's actually gone.

Many survivors find that they didn't really know how to express sadness or anger throughout most of their lives. They were instead expected to be a cheerful servant for everyone around them. And so they developed this stubborn light in their hearts that always sought to see the best in everything, no matter what evidence pointed to the contrary.

But you will come to see that the psychopath is something that your heart can never light up. And you will try. That's what cognitive dissonance is all about. For months, you oscillated back and forth between the idealize and devalue phases, trying to understand which one was real. You reasoned that of course they loved you, because they said they did. But then you looked at their actions, which did not at all reflect their words. You know intuitively that love is not insulting, criticizing, cheating, and lying. Love does not make you feel suicidal. Love does not mock you for having hurt feelings.

And so, the more you thought about it, the angrier and more depressed you got. The light inside of you began to fade away as this person consumed your every thought. The light could not transform their behavior, so instead it started to absorb it, growing dimmer every day.

As time went on, you felt profound rage and emptiness that you'd never felt in your life. Throughout most of the process, you probably didn't even know how to express it. So on the outside, you remained this happy person that everyone expected and needed. You wouldn't want to inconvenience anyone with your feelings. But deep down, something was changing. The light was almost out, and suddenly you found yourself feeling very resentful and irritated with many people—people you thought were your closest friends.

After each interaction, you'd return home and find yourself reflecting for hours on what had just taken place. Who was that? It wasn't you. You didn't truly believe the things you were saying, and you certainly held no respect for the gossip and insults they so adored. Suddenly your light isn't justifying it all away as humor anymore. You're just left with the cold reality that you've surrounded yourself with some very unkind people.

You're left as a drained battery that's still expected to fuel a rocket. Your energy is broken. You want to automatically love everyone like you used to, but you can't. Unkindness and superficiality frustrate you when they never did before.

For a long time, you probably remembered the psychopath so fondly not because they were a good person, but because that was the peak of your light. You were rewarded every single day for denying the bad and glorifying the mediocre. You now associate that relationship with your light, but that does not mean they actually made you happy. It means your innocence made you happy, because it was protecting your very gentle heart.

Coming to disassociate your innocence with genuine happiness is essential to your healing process. Simply because you once felt euphoric with the psychopath and friends who frequently insulted you does not mean that life was actually great at the time. Likewise, just because you feel sadness now does not mean that your life is somehow bad. On the contrary, things are looking brighter than ever before. You're just struggling to enjoy the world without your light.

But you don't have to. Your light never left you—it's just waiting. Yes, it's a bit shy right now. But as you begin to develop your self-respect and boundaries, the light will flicker back on. And as you explore your love & spirituality, the light will return stronger than ever.

So many survivors long for when life was "normal" and "happy", but how much of that was ever real? How much of that was really spent by you desperately trying to replace the negative with positive? How much of it was projection, while other people were busy projecting their own poison onto you? When your light fades, especially after a trauma like this, it becomes far more difficult to keep projecting goodness onto others.

So I believe that you do not truly miss your past, but instead the light you associate with it.

One thing I've noticed about every member on PsychopathFree.com is that none of them want to feel this darkness. Not a single one. They do not want to be victims. They want to recover their happiness and joy. They feel this burning anger that they are even angry in the first place. They've practiced forgiveness throughout their entire lives, only to be confronted with the most unforgivable experience of a psychopath. Why? What was the point? Why did your identity need to be destroyed like this, leaving you so incredibly broken and drained?

With time, you will find your own answers to these questions. Your innocence was a beautiful gift, but the paradox was that you never knew you had it. This was why you tended to pour so much of your love and affection into other human beings. Because you hadn't yet felt that love for yourself. Through the psychopathic healing process, you make that final leap. As uncomfortable as it may be, you find self-respect and begin creating healthy boundaries. Instead of trying to fit in with others, you find yourself wondering why people don't behave more like you. Empathetic, compassionate, loving, outgoing, creative, easy-going, responsible, caring... The gentle souls who walk this Earth and touch it only with kindness.

When your light is gone, you can no longer use it to fix all of the broken things around you. So in its place, you begin to surround yourself with people who actually share and appreciate your most wonderful qualities. And you can't discover all of that magic until your innocence is gone, giving you an opportunity to see the world as it truly is—as you truly are.

This journey is about you, and it always has been. Once you discover this, you are finally ready to fly free.

FREEDOM

You can free your spirit with the very same imagination you once used to imprison it. With this knowledge, you take full responsibility for the person you're about to become.

Looking Back

Once you have truly and completely disconnected your spirit from the psychopath, you will be able to look back on the experience from a less emotional perspective. You will begin to understand that you are not missing out on anything—in fact, you got lucky.

I know it doesn't seem like that at first. It always feels like they're winning, because that's the image they share with the world. You're left thinking that they've pranced off into the sunset with some other partner, but you've forgotten about something very important. How can any single human being go from such horrifying abuse, to a sudden & perfect relationship with someone else? They can't. It's emotionally and logically impossible.

Sure, you might wish they'd break up, just for the validation. But it won't make any difference. The psychopath will repeat their cycle until the day they die or settle down with a comfortable target. You do not need to stick around and watch. They'll maintain the shallow illusion of success &

happiness, no matter what happens. You will never gain any satisfaction from their downfall. Instead, you will come to understand that their entire life is a failure—a sham

No matter how much they screw up, they will always pass off their pathetic behavior as comedy—a mask to minimize their failures. They pretend that their mistakes are intentional, constantly redefining the rules of a game that no one wanted to play in the first place. You do not need to take part in these imaginary competitions. You have already won. It's the psychopath who fails, every time. DawnG authored this unforgettable article on PsychopathFree.com:

On Psychopaths & Winning

"The psychopath had you and lost you. They lost your love, your devotion, your care and concern. They did this with deception, betrayal, and abuse. This is no win.

They use people and throw them out like yesterday's garbage. They will never maintain lasting and true friendships with healthy people. Their families give up on them or, even worse, keep spending their precious love and energy bailing them out of trouble and protecting them from the consequences of their own actions. Does this sound like a win for anyone?

They don't know what love is. They will never know what it is like to make love with someone they truly love. They will never know joy at creating a life with a partner. They will never have that connection with other human beings. They will never know what it's like to look at their children's faces and feel overwhelming and unconditional love. They will never understand those feelings of helplessness when one of their children, a parent, or a spouse becomes ill. They will never rejoice when the illness is cured.

They will never feel empathy for another human being. They will never see suffering in the world and feel that determination to make it a better place for everyone.

A psychopath will never feel that sense of accomplishment at a job well done. They spend their lives always scheming, working angles, manipulating people and situations. They are never satisfied with what they have. There always has to be more, better. They usually **fail** because they simply can't get it right. And then they blame others for their failures. That lack of personal insight is no win. It guarantees that they will never grow and learn as people.

But you—you are none of these things. You have insight, and you had the determination to want to figure out what in the world happened to you.

You might be out of this horrible relationship, or at least are strongly thinking about it. You're learning, growing, helping yourself

That's a win. You win.

They lose. Always."

Introspection & Insecurities

During and after the relationship, you're a victim of abuse. You were manipulated, insulted, degraded, belittled, and neglected. Full responsibility for this goes to the psychopath. It does not matter if you were vulnerable or insecure—no decent human being should ever take advantage of another. None of that was your fault.

But there comes a point where must begin to hold yourself accountable. This generally occurs once you've educated yourself, learned the signs, and validated your experience—after you've found a comfortable landing spot from the stages of grief. When you get to this point, you should be disgusted by the psychopath's behavior and have no desire to see or hear from them again.

You cannot continue to question yourself, fantasizing about returning to them and seeking validation for self-destructive decisions. This book and the PsychopathFree forum are not crutches—they are stepping stones. Sooner or later, all survivors must learn to make decisions on their own, without seeking the opinions of everyone around them. Better life choices can only truly come from within, and you will know when you're making them because your intuition & self-respect will skyrocket. You certainly won't need to seek any external approval.

Introspection is a great way to look within and discover why you're looking for this approval in the first place. It could be rooted in your childhood, past friendships, the psychopathic relationship—or any combination of the above. In order to better understand how all of this came to be, you can look back on the relationship and examine the toxic dynamic that formed. The psychopath's mirroring techniques are actually an incredible, once-in-a-lifetime opportunity to take a look at your own demons.

Mirror, Mirror on the Wall

It's time to start asking questions. Why did this happen? What are your vulnerabilities? Of course these vulnerabilities aren't your fault, but it is important to understand how you were able to be exploited. This will help you to further deconstruct the bond with them, and protect yourself from any future emotional abuse.

This experience is all about cultivating a healthy self-esteem that comes from within, not from any sort of external validation. We all have insecurities and vanities—many of which we're probably not aware of. True self-discovery comes from practicing introspection and becoming aware of those characteristics.

This part is really up to you, but here are some of the most common answers for survivors: looks, humor, money, career, an unfulfilling marriage, need for attention, need to be appreciated, fear of being alone...

Look at your relationship with the psychopath. They regurgitated these insecurities for you. Whatever you needed most, they validated and provided. Pay special attention to the things they obsessively flattered. These are what you're looking for.

So what are your insecurities? Get out a piece of paper and make a list. This will save your life down the road. Once you're aware of these traits, you will also become aware of the people who try to manipulate them. And even better, you can begin to make changes—to better yourself and improve your life. For example, why should you need someone else to tell you you're attractive in order to feel it in your heart?

Those who have conquered their demons will be completely useless to a psychopath. You won't be susceptible to the psychopath's grooming if you do not require validation, but instead simply enjoy a compliment every now and then. Psychopaths feed on unhealthy needs, not everyday kindness. With time, you will find yourself less and less attracted to those who excessively flatter and praise you.

Keep in mind, there is another kind of vulnerability: the good kind. Your dreams—sexual fantasies, life goals, romantic endeavors, perhaps raising a family… These are all beautiful, good vulnerabilities that make you human. Do not let the psychopathic experience change these things. Next to your list of insecurities, make a list of your dreams. You must never mistake your passions for flaws. And likewise, your empathetic nature is not a weakness—although the psychopath certainly makes you question that.

Sympathy for the Devil

Cute. Adorable. Baby. You'll often hear these adjectives used to describe a psychopath. It's all part of the charm. You were probably never attracted to arrogance, jerks, and over-confidence. Instead, you're drawn to the innocent, sympathetic partner—the one who tells you you're making them happier than anyone else. There is a strange pattern among most survivors: going from "giving them attention" to "needing their attention" in the blink of an eye. How did this transition happen? How did you lose your self-esteem to someone who seemed to have none to begin with?

When you first met the psychopath, you probably felt sorry for them. They had so many sympathetic qualities: their ex had abused them, they were insecure about the way they looked, they'd been so unhappy until they met you, and now they can't believe they're dating someone in your league.

This is where your empathy kicks in. You've done it all your life: you see someone feeling inferior, and you know how to make them feel better. You want to heal them. And so you put yourself down to raise someone else up.

The psychopath is like no one else, because they genuinely seem to adore all of your efforts. They compare you to past exes, idealizing you above everyone else. It's as if all of your energies finally have a purpose, after likely being frustrated with the unending, not-so-appreciative complaints of friends and family members. Remember all of this from earlier?

Many survivors report not even being attracted to the psychopath at first. But with time, you begin to see them as the best looking person in the world. You can't even think of anyone else sexually. How did this happen?

By pouring all of your empathetic capital into healing their supposed insecurities, you come to a point where you actually start to believe your own kindness & compassion. You become obsessed with proving your loyalty, because you believe the problem is their insecurity. If you make yourself vulnerable enough, surely they will learn to overcome their inferiority complex.

But that's not the problem and it never was.

You know now that you spent all this time chasing a manufactured illusion: you were under the impression that they thought they were lucky to be with you. You probably didn't like that power dynamic, so you built up your partner in order to make them feel better. And this is how they hooked you: with sympathy. If you perceive them as child-like, your natural instincts kick in, and you do everything you can to prove how much you care. This is likely the way you've dealt with people throughout your entire life: when others have no self-confidence, you try to build it for them.

Like a psychopath, you can probably sense insecurities. The difference lies in how you act upon those insecurities. Psychopaths see them as a way to manipulate & control. Empathetic people, on the other hand, seek to cure insecurities with love and compassion. This is why so many survivors find themselves surrounded with negative people after the breakup. Because for a long time, you probably gained your sense of self-worth from making miserable people happy.

So when the psychopath came along, you had more self-worth than ever before, because it was dependent on others. You experienced chemical changes, forming an immediate bond of love & trust. You were willing to do whatever it took to build up their happiness. You constantly complimented their looks, you didn't mind paying for dates, you laughed at their jokes even when they weren't funny. And in return, you were rewarded with their overwhelming appreciation that gave your life meaning.

But somewhere in this whirlwind, you suddenly found the tables turned. It happened fast. Instead of sympathetically reassuring the poor guy/girl, you found yourself desperate for **their** approval.

They began to make it clear that they did not actually need all of that attention. In fact, they found it very annoying. When you complimented them, you received an arrogant laugh or a disingenuous "you too baby". It's as if you became the relationship newbie, and they were the one who would take things from there.

Additionally, the attention started coming from other sources. Your unique ability to make them happy wasn't so unique after all. This triangulation was pure torture.

They used the silent treatment to punish you and deride your once-needed sympathies. You began to feel stupid, unattractive, needy, and useless. Your solution was to continue self-destructing to make room for their "feelings". You brushed aside complaints of their lying or triangulating because they made it very clear that this kind of talk was unacceptable.

Do you see what happened? The ball was in their court. And the scary thing is, despite your own beliefs, it was never in your court to begin with. All they did was make you believe it was. By giving you this false sense of self-confidence and importance, you opened up fast. This is why you trusted the psychopath very quickly and let them into your life without a second guess.

This is also why the grand finale was more terrible than anything you've ever felt before. It was the outright dismissal of your self-worth. You invested all of it in them, thereby giving them the power to take it away. You never even comprehended a power struggle, because you were too busy pleasing their invented baby persona. After all, how in the world could a baby be plotting manipulation & domination? It's as if they declared "checkmate" when you thought you were playing checkers.

And you were addicted to more than just their attention—you also became addicted to their approval of your attention. You felt empty without it, and that's why a psychopathic breakup takes so long to recover from. You are not just getting over a romantic encounter; you're rebuilding your self-worth from scratch. That's why you become so sensitive to the reactions of future partners. Until you go through the recovery process, you will be bouncing around trying to find a replacement for that approval—something to give your life meaning again.

But there is good news here, and it outweighs everything else. Once you begin recovery, your life changes forever. You start to find overwhelming self-worth in your own values, behavior, and heart. Remember those negative people I mentioned above? Slowly but surely, they begin to disappear from the picture. At first, you question yourself and remember how "happy" you were with them. But as you redefine your self-worth, you come to realize that **you** created this happiness. And similar to your relationship with the psychopath, you thought these people needed your happiness. Well, this isn't your responsibility anymore. You have better things coming your way.

Self-Respect

Instead of trying to gain everyone else's approval, you will at some point find yourself wondering why people can't be more like you. Why can't they be easy-going, kind, caring, selfless, accommodating, and self-aware? This is called self-respect. This is your self-worth coming from within. Of course it still feels good to make someone else happy, but now you have a much better measure of who deserves your light. And this will bring you joy for the rest of your life.

You will also begin to discover that the psychopath targeted you specifically because of these assets. This does not make them weaknesses—all you needed was the self-awareness and self-respect to take pride in them. To quote my honorary Aunt Peru: "They are fascinated with human emotion and are forever honing their craft of mimicking 'normal'. Empathetic people have the full spectrum of emotions so it's like a master class for them. Also, they can suck these people of the life force they lack—giving and trusting, we make perfect targets."

And of course, there is nothing wrong with being giving and trusting. Self-respect is simply about coming to expect the same thing from others. This is when you begin to discover all of your strengths. Many of these were qualities you always possessed but never valued. You realize that your compassion, empathy, and love are not weaknesses. They are the most incredible gifts in the world, when applied to the right people. You start to understand who you're truly meant to be. It took the psychopath's cruelty to make you see exactly who you never want to be. You laugh at their old notions that "you are the same person", because you realize you are exactly the opposite. You begin to explore your creative side, and you stop caring what others think of you. Old friendships may also start to change as you change and become more confident. Your boundaries are returning, or perhaps being formed for the very first time.

Boundaries

Building boundaries is one of the most difficult parts about developing self-respect. It feels unnatural, almost psychopathic at first. How can you be strict with people who need your help? And moreover, how do you deal with those who accuse you of hypersensitivity because you're no longer their doormat?

One of the kindest members I've ever had the pleasure of knowing, Wakeup, had some great thoughts on this: "Some seem to believe that women who have been devastated from romantic involvement with psychopaths are back lashing against good men, and thereby probably missing out on good relationships by being hypersensitive and overly careful.

I have a different take on this. I don't want to exclude the men who suffer from same sex or opposite sex psychopaths, so I include them as well. Rather than it being a compensatory mechanism, being very careful about potential future romantic (and I would include non-romantic) relationships is a necessary evolution toward critical thinking, a waking up from being brainwashed—often from our family of origin and certainly from our culture. This 'waking up' is often very uncomfortable, and it takes a lot more energy and effort to think and evaluate the process of bringing others closer to our lives. But is also absolutely necessary for personal development on all levels."

You must come to differentiate hypersensitivity from having healthy boundaries. The people who accuse you of being unreasonable are very likely to be abrasive, rude, or unpleasant themselves. The only difference is, now you're not their doormat. They will do whatever they can to maintain the existing dynamic, because more boundaries means less complacency. You should never feel the need to defend yourself against a friend. You should never have to explain why you can't make plans one evening. And you should never be walking on eggshells, trying to rephrase a text to avoid an unpleasant interaction.

These people-pleasing habits are toxic to you, and often stem from a past need to make others happy. But sometimes, there isn't any deeper origin to these patterns beyond simply being a gentle person. If you naturally tend to be agreeable & friendly, toxic people will sense this and latch onto you. They quickly discover how to manipulate you with guilt-tripping, passive aggression, and martyrdom. This snowballs, as more and more of these people find you. You become stuck in their cycles of insecurity, which is often the reason you're already desensitized to the psychopath's abuse.

You should always feel comfortable sitting down with a friend and mentioning a concern. Normal people are receptive to self-improvement, especially if it's phrased kindly. Empathetic people should be especially invested in making sure they haven't hurt your feelings. But toxic people will instead blow up, turning the conversation back on you. Or they'll blame their past and offer up fake apologies, only to continue the exact same behavior the following week. If you find yourself repeatedly excusing someone else's bad behavior, stop and consider why **they** shouldn't simply behave in a way that doesn't require excusing to begin with.

Channeling Empathy

Survivors should never shutdown their empathy as a coping mechanism for abuse. Instead, their special abilities should be saved for those who can truly appreciate & reciprocate them. Your Constant is probably an example of one of these people. Abusers, on the other hand, manipulate your greatest qualities and make you doubt yourself. So how can you live healthily in a world where you are bound to encounter both good and bad people every day? How can you stand up for yourself, and still retain a strong sense of your gentle, compassionate nature? The answer lies in learning to "channel" your empathy—to disconnect from toxic people, and not feel bad for doing so.

The loss of innocence is your heart's way of beginning this path. Now that you're learning to discover who's healthy and who's not, you understand that you are not obligated to make everyone around you happy. You can find the greatest peace by surrounding yourself with a small, trusted group of warmhearted people. Then, you will be free to exercise all of your compassion, without feeling exhausted & drained.

Around toxic people, however, you will start to put these abilities on hold. This doesn't mean you somehow become a temporary psychopath (is there even such a thing?). All you're doing is protecting your spirit. This means perceiving with your brain, instead of your heart. Your heart will always be ready to trust and believe the best in others. But your brain will provide you with a logical, emotionally disconnected assessment of the situation. This is the best way to deal with toxic people. You do not need to waste your emotional capital on them. You only have so much, and you deserve to spend it on the people who make you happy.

The Psychopath Free Pledge

When members first join our forum, we ask them to take a pledge. It's a promise that honors self-respect and encourages healthy relationships. If you follow these simple points, you will find permanent freedom from toxic bonds:

1. I will never beg or plead for someone else again. Any man or woman who brings me to that level is not worth my heart.
2. I will never tolerate criticisms about my body, age, weight, job, or any other insecurities I might have. Good partners won't put me down, they'll raise me up.
3. I will take a step back from my relationship once every month to make sure that I am being respected and loved, not flattered and love-bombed.
4. I will always ask myself the question: "Would I ever treat someone else like this?" If the answer is no, then I don't deserve to be treated like that either.
5. I will trust my gut. If I get a bad feeling, I won't try to push it away and make excuses. I will trust myself.
6. I understand that it is better to be single than in a toxic relationship.
7. I will not be spoken to in a condescending or sarcastic way. Loving partners will not patronize me.

8. I will not allow my partner to call me jealous, crazy, or any other form of projection.
9. My relationships will be mutual and equal at all times. Love is not about control and power.
10. If I ever feel unsure about any of these steps, I will seek out help from a friend, support forum, or therapist. I will not act on impulsive decisions.

Do you take the pledge? If so, sign your name on this page as a reminder—so you can come back any time and re-member the promise you made to yourself. Treating yourself kindly not only accelerates the healing process, it also sets healthier habits in motion that will carry on throughout your future relationships and friendships. So do yourself a favor, and train your mind to start expecting the good things you've always deserved.

Authenticity

The recovery process is the beginning of your new life. You'll look back at old dynamics, wondering how you ever tolerated such toxicity. As I mentioned earlier, you might even feel embarrassed about your past behavior. This "re-gret" is your self-respect kicking in, reminding you that you're different now.

After the relationship, you probably felt yourself "cheer-leading" a lot, disingenuously handing out compliments as a way to receive them back yourself. With time, these start to become much more personal and sincere. You develop strong friendships with people that you truly care about, in-stead of just selflessly throwing yourself at every survivor you meet along the way. This is **healthy**. The world is a big place.

You shouldn't be best friends with everyone you come across. It's far better to have a few good friends than a million acquaintances with whom you exchange shallow formalities.

Along those same lines, survivors who spend their days helping others should be proud of themselves. Whether it be online, in person, or over the phone, you're doing something incredible to change the world. Abuse recovery is a part of who you are, and you should feel comfortable sharing this with friends & partners. You work with survivors, and that's a passion worth mentioning.

As you become your most genuine self, the people around you will not-so-coincidentally start to transform as well. Enjoy this, and don't forget to credit yourself for all of the hard work you've done to make it a reality.

Spirituality & Love

Once you have self-respect, you are free to become who you were always meant to be. You do not care about the petty judgments of others, giving you the opportunity to fully explore your creativity, imagination, and spirituality.

This is where the magic begins.

Embrace the new you, and open your heart to love again. You should be so, incredibly proud of yourself. You made it, and your life path has forever changed for the better. You might encounter toxic people, but you know you'll never fall for one again. Your mind, heart, and body have all aligned, rendering you invincible to the mind games of the soulless.

You no longer waste your time ruminating on the past, because the present & future are so much brighter. Instead of analyzing the sketchy behavior of others, you stop yourself immediately and simply remove them from your life. You know better now.

Your spirit wakes up after years of hibernation, ready to take on the world & connect with this great universe. You have an important place here, and you always have. You do things for **you**, not to impress others. Our administrator & friend, MorningAfter, wrote one of the most touching pieces I've ever seen. In my eyes, this is the true face of healing:

Slowly But Surely

"I used to get into a panic if my phone didn't ring on weekends. Now I get into panic if it does.

I used to feel sad and lonely if I didn't go out—now, I need more time alone because of so many books I want to read, things I want to do in my flat, hours I want to spend walking... My day needs to be longer.

I used to be so self-centered in how I look, I used to wear uncomfortable shoes with high heels on my way to work. Today I went to the office and I went for a jogging and I felt good. Wearing high heels makes me feel better, but if I can't feel good with myself in old jeans, the best dress won't help me.

I used to have make up always... Now it is not relevant. I appreciate people smiling more than before. I feel more connected with people now than before...

I see people walking and smiling and I spend a second thinking about them and I feel happy for them.

There is sadness also. But it is what life is made of. Both good and bad things. But how I feel them, makes a difference.

My fear is that I will not make close friendships and close relationships anymore. But I am just walking one third of the average recovery path, so who can know what will wait for me in future. I am afraid of relying on somebody... but the beauty I am discovering now is to rely on myself. For the very first time in my life. And to have a good time doing that.

Thank you all for being a part of that change and for helping me set up better standards for myself. Sometimes it appears to be lonely here where I am, but that conclusion is based upon my old type of thinking. I am not lonely, I just cleared up my life from miserable and mean people, and I have space left for new good people and good things to come into my life.

Slowly but surely."

Gratitude & Forgiveness

During the healing process, we often lose sight of how much good there is in the world. But it is there, from the moment you wake up in the morning to the last thought you have before drifting off to sleep. All you have to do is open your heart to it.

Every day, amazing things are happening. People are laughing, birds flying, children playing, waves crashing... What an enchanting life this is! But when we spend time focusing on the very few things that aren't going well, we lose sight of what really matters—we forget how to be happy.

I would like to share a practice that has helped me cultivate gratitude over the past few years. It might not work for you, but it brings so much peace to my heart. Before going to sleep each night, I think about someone I am grateful for. It is usually my mom or a close friend. I imagine their face, their smile, and their genuine goodness.

I bow to their spirit, and then I repeat this process for another trusted spirit. And another. And another. I am always surprised to find that this activity never ends. I have never reached "the end" before falling asleep, because I do not believe there is a tangible end to all the good people in this world.

Some survivors, myself included, place a great deal of importance in the idea of forgiveness. With the above activity, you can slowly start to integrate the people who have hurt you into your peaceful thoughts. It will feel wrong at first, and you might get triggered by the very idea of them. But slowly, they will find a soft place in your heart. How could they not, when surrounded by so much love?

Do not mistake forgiveness for contact. Just because you forgive the psychopath does not mean they should ever have a place in your life again. And you certainly should not feel the need to tell them that you've forgiven them. True forgiveness comes from within, not from another person validating your compassion.

If you choose not to forgive the psychopath, that's fine too. Some survivors feel that this would be an insult to their soul, and I completely understand. This is your decision, and I could never hope to understand the inner-workings of someone else's heart. Do whatever brings you the most happiness—only you will know how to do that.

The Angel

To be honest, I thought the Spirituality section of this chapter would be much longer. But I quickly came to realize that spirituality is the most personal journey in the human experience. And so how in the world could I hope to offer any sort of advice about it?

Well, I did try for a little bit—and I failed. So instead, I'll just quickly tell you about a spiritual experience of my own.

One day, my gentle & wise friend, Iris, sent me a tiny angel figurine from across the world. It arrived during a difficult time in my life, and it was completely unexpected. The gesture alone was enough to bring tears to my eyes. Over the next several months, I carried the angel with me everywhere. And slowly, I found that my life seemed to be repairing itself.

I was smiling on the way to work again. I was calling friends & family just to hear their voices. And at night, I was dreaming to the quiet sounds of nature. I knew that everything would be okay. Someone was keeping me safe.

Later in the year, the angel found a new home. My brother had been struggling with drug addiction for over four years. On a particularly snowy evening, I got a call that he was in the emergency room—he had tried to kill himself. I will never forget holding his hand in the hospital that night. I wanted more than anything to keep him safe. But I felt completely useless, unable to do anything helpful. And so I slipped the angel into his hands and told him that she would keep him safe.

Months later, he was released from rehabilitation. And from the moment I saw his eyes, I knew he had healed. I saw the brother that I hadn't seen in four years.

And so you see, the kind gift of a friend touched our family in a way that I can never explain. Because spirituality cannot be explained—only felt. This is why I try never be dismissive of someone else's beliefs. If it makes them happy (and does not infringe upon anyone else's happiness), then it is good. I personally find so much joy in the fact that we are all inter-connected by something amazing. I don't know what it is, but I love it.

So, what about you? Maybe you find spirituality in religion, the supernatural, exercise, friendship, family, stuffed animals, music, pets, painting, or gardening. Or maybe, you are still searching. Actually, I suppose we all are. And that's the best part about being human, isn't it?

Finding Love Again

Surprisingly enough, love and sex after psychopathic recovery is better than ever before. Unlike anything you've ever experienced. You were originally conditioned to feel addicted to desperation & intense passion—something you once mistook for love. But now, you know better. Love is gentle, patient, and kind. Love is consistent and creative. You do not doubt your partner's intentions. Instead, two spirits peacefully coexist, exploring the world together.

Depending on your abusive past, you may need time to work through some sexual triggers. A truly good partner will give you all the time in the world. They will communicate & empathize, ensuring that you feel comfortable no matter what. Instead of sex being used as a tool for manipulation, you will find that normal, healthy partners have sex as a way to bond and express love for one another.

Once you're able to trust fully, your physical and emotional intimacy will blossom like a flower—growing and maturing from the past. You're finally able to apply all the things you've been learning throughout the healing process. You know what you deserve, and you know who you are. You are able to freely give your loving energy because it's respected & cherished, instead of being wasted on a black hole.

With psychopaths, you never know where you stand. You live in a constant state of uncertainty, wondering each day whether or not they care about you. Your entire life is consumed by this day-by-day struggle. But with real love, all of this garbage is forgotten. You do not question yourself. It is a mutual partnership of dedication and passion.

There is something truly amazing about meeting the right person and finally realizing, "Wow, they are never going to abuse me." Think about that for a moment. You dealt with months—probably years—of emotional abuse, and now you've worked so hard that everything has changed. You **ended** the cycle of emotional violence, all on your own. You uprooted your patterns and redefined your life's path. And as a reward, your heart is finally free.

Do not worry about when this will happen. When the time is right, someone will come along and recognize all of the greatness within you. And what's more, you will know in your heart when you've found the one. There is no rush.

You know that feeling you get when you discover a great song and you listen to it on repeat all day, wondering how you ever went a day in your life without hearing it? Love is sort of like that. It pops up out of nowhere, and before you know it, you're singing along for the rest of your life.

AFTERWORD
The Constant: Revisited

What an adventure this has been. I'm sitting here with three cats & a hot cup of coffee, wondering why it took me so long to mention my cats. Sometimes they are my Constant. Sometimes my mom is my Constant. Sometimes memories from Singing Beach are my Constant. Sometimes the members of PsychopathFree are my Constant.

Accidentally, it would seem that everyone in my life has become a Constant.

But back to my cats. I like to go for winter walks in the snow with them. They're weird, sort of like dogs, following the tracks I make out in the woods. Earlier this morning, we spent a long time out there, exploring and dreaming together. We discovered new & untold secrets of the universe. We learned about growing up and trusting love again. We found hope in the goodness of mankind. We saw Light and Dark, battling each other throughout all of eternity.

It was in that moment that I realized something: I am my own Constant. I love my quiet time alone. I love existing here in this mysterious world. I love being a part of something so much bigger than myself. And I love not having a clue what comes next.

But above all, I love that adversity has introduced me to some of the most incredible human beings this world has to offer. There is something connecting all of us, I am sure of it. And because of the friendships, I would not change this experience. Not in a million years.

Our adventure is only just beginning—and now that our hearts have healed, it's time to start some trouble. Or at least, that's what the cats are telling me.

8101373R00085